The Latin American short-story in the 20th Century

Translation by Jesús Daniel Ovallos

PALABRA ESCRITA

The diversity of the Latin American short stories

In the month of June in 2015, after publishing *El cuento fantástico en el Río de la Plata* (*The fantastic short-story in Río de la Plata*), I committed myself to keep working on literary essays, about short-story writers who had ventured into the fantasy genre, but this time, not only in the region of Río de la Plata; I was interested in extending those examinations in order to study different authors, starting with the Latin American ones. About the writers from my country, I had already worked on *El almohadón de plumas* (*The feather pillow*) by Horacio Quiroga, a short story about the unexplainable death of a woman after being attacked by a strange animal that lives in a pillow; I also had published two studies about Felisberto Hernández: one about the upholders and the detractors of his works, and another which approaches a literary analysis of the short story *Muebles: el canario* (*The canary: Furniture shop*), a wonderful narration in which, in a very fantastic way, makes a ruthless critic to the media in service to the commercial advertising. I also had already worked on some writers who had approached the fantastic genre in Argentina. I had published a study about "El Aleph", by Jorge Luis Borges, a story which main topic is the clash between one single person and the infinite, represented in an object; and, at last, with occasion of the Julio Cortazar's one hundredth's birthday, I published a study about *La continuidad de los parques* (*Continuity of the parks*), his terrific story in which the writer moves around the different levels of fiction with incommensurable mastery. One of the fantastic short stories I have always liked, which has had a great impact on me since the first time I read it was *El guardagujas* (*The switchman*), by Mexican writer Juan José Arreola, so I continued my essay journey about Latin American short-story writers with that text. *The switchman* is a story that allows a multiplicity of interpretations, some more evident than others, but there we can appreciate a satire about the Mexican railroad system; a critic to dehumanizing mercantilism; an allegory about the fate of mankind; an absurd look to some political systems and social institutions; a great work indeed. After working in the story of Arreola, I decided to change my primary plans, I would no longer continue to look for stories with fantastic characteristics throughout the American continent, but I would choose the stories that I considered the best or more representative of each country. I realized that I would have chosen the foretold stories and put them in a selection of the best Latin American short stories of the past century. If I reduced my search specter only to those stories which held fantastic characteristics, I would be taking the risk of choosing stories of a minor quality because, as I expressed in the prologue of *The fantastic short story in the Río de la Plata*, that characteristic was more intense in the Río de la Plata than in the rest of Latin America. Thus, I decided to change the main project, which was writing a big essay about the fantastic short stories in Latin America (a job very unlikely to be finished, if you ask me), to a more ambitious and subjective one, writing a work about the best short stories and short story writers in Latin America in the 20th century.

Now that the work is complete, I see that it can be divided into four thematic blocks, something that wasn't initially planned. We have the block concerning the aforementioned five stories. A second block consisting in short stories about the teenager world. These tales are: *Clandestine happiness* by Clarice Lispector, a story about evil, moral suffering and the humiliation of a young girl in the hands of a girl from her same school; *Día domingo* (*On Sunday*) by Mario Vargas Llosa, a short story about the clash between two young boys for the love of a girl; in the end, we'll approach *Un regalo para Julia* (*A gift for Julia*) by Francisco Massiani, which shares the teenager thematic with the other stories, but focuses in the insecurities and uncertainties of the aforementioned period of the life. The third block consists in only two short stories which axis is the *Guerra del Chaco* (Chaco War), a war that faced Bolivians and Paraguayans between 1932 and 1935. One of this tales is *La excavación* (*The excavation*) by Augusto Roa Bastos, a tale that narrates the agonic struggle of a man trying to achieve his freedom, in which he references both the internal Paraguayan wars and the mentioned Chaco War. The other short story in this block approaches the other side of the war, from the Bolivian side. I am talking about a story named *El pozo* (*The well*), a short story about the despair and hope of a group of bolivian soldiers who protect a barren well in which they try to get water from, uselessly, but for which they are willing to give their lives if necessary, in a totally useless war, like the Chaco War itself. Finally, in the fourth and last block of studied short stories, we will take a look into the works of three authors with an own characteristic voice that makes them different from the rest of the other writers. Here we will see *Sensini*, probably the most recognized and representative story by Roberto Bolaño about literary creation and literary contests. It is a text which unveils the struggling reality that exiled non consecrated writers have to coup in the small towns' literary contests, which is not glory and recognizement, but just an economical relief that allows them to ease their daily needs. Another author with an own voice, that we can appreciate in this block of arbitrary classifying I decided to establish, is Gabriel García Márquez. From the Colombian author, I chose to analyze a tale titled *Un día de estos* (*One of these days*), included in his first short stories book *Los funerales de la Mamá Grande* (*Big Mama's funeral*). It is a tale that shows a truce established in the ideological conflict between the people (represented by a dentist) and the Government (represented by a Mayor) and the reversion of roles in which the people, at least for a short moment, impose their rules. The last text in this block is *Un hombre muerto a puntapiés* (*A man dead by kicks*), written by the best Ecuadorian short story writer ever, Pablo Palacio. It is a story in which the main topic is the aggression, the violent behavior and the social problems deriving from the reluctance to accept different sexual preferences in the city of Quito by the times in which the author lived.

Fernando Chelle

HORACIO QUIROGA

The feather pillow

A short story about madness love and, above all, Death

By: Fernando Chelle

The text chosen for the literary analysis is by Uruguayan writer Horacio Quiroga (Salto, Uruguay, December 31st 1878 - Buenos Aires, Argentina, February 18th 1937). It is a short story titled *El almohadón de plumas* (*The feather pillow*), included in the book *Cuentos de amor, de locura y de muerte* (*Tales of love, madness and death*) published in Buenos Aires in 1917.

The main topic in this story is the unexplainable death of Alicia, the protagonist, victim of a strange animal that lives in her feather pillow. The other two topics seen in the title of the book, love and madness, are present in the story, but just in a supporting way.

Quiroga chose to structure the action in a similar way as Edgar Allan Poe did in many of his Extraordinary Tales, in which we can find the so-called effect endings, precisely because of the impression meant to be caused in the reader. As in *The black cat*, to mention just one story by the North American author, in *The feather pillow*, the writer keeps the ace in his sleeve until he reaches the end of the story, in order to surprise the reader. This short story is structured in a classical form, that is, beginning, development and end. The first moment of the story is dedicated to showing the characters and the place where the story is happening: the house. The second moment, the longest one, rolls around the protagonist's newly acquired and unexplainable sickness; and lastly, there is a third moment which focuses on the feather pillow and the strange animal living inside of it, which ends up being the cause of Alicia's death.

The story begins with a convincing sentence, loaded with an oxymoronic meaning: "*Her honeymoon was a long cold shudder*". As readers, we know that the honeymoon is the period that starts once a wedding is over and goes on for a lapse of time, in which, generally, the just married couple goes on a vacation trip. It is a moment of intimacy distinctive for being a time of intense happiness. When we read the first words of the text, we can already notice the tone of the story; we know nothing about it yet, but one thing is clear: a honeymoon does not have the distinction of being a cold shudder.

The omniscient third person narrative voice keeps defining the graphopoetic (physical characteristics) and etopoetic (character features) features of the two main characters. About Alicia, we are told that she is blonde, angelical and shy, while Jordan is described as a tall, silent and rough man. Quiroga's intention in this first moment of the story is to show the relationship of a couple who love each other, but marked by the lack of communication. We are told that Alicia loves Jordan a lot and that he loves her very much as well, but that Alicia somehow feels scared in front of the rigid presence of her husband, she is not even able to look at him in the eye; and Jordan, in his muteness, is unable to let his feelings known.

With the description of the house, the physical place where the events are going to happen, the writer tries (and succeeds) to get the attention of the reader to different interpretations of what will happen to the protagonist. The house is said to be hostile and described as a haunted, cold and abandoned palace which has an influence on the psychological aspect of the protagonist.

In the planning of the tale, Quiroga knows beforehand the way and the circumstances in which Alicia is going to die, but he has to create some transitory interpretations for the readers about the facts happening during the reading so, when the truth about Alicia's sickness comes out and the real cause of her death is revealed, there is a total surprise. In that vein, it's logical to think that Alicia's shudders, that will end up being a strange sickness, are caused by the circumstances around her, like being married to a not very communicative man and living in isolation in that weird house, giving up her sensitive woman's dreams.

When the narrator says that "*It is not strange that she grew thin*", the first reference to a probable illness, we are not surprised, even if at this point, we are too far to know the real cause of it.

The illness of the protagonist began as a simple flu, but it becomes bizarre as she is not getting over it, and her health keeps declining.

The part in the garden, in which Jordan caresses Alicia's head and she starts crying, is very significant. This is the only moment in the story where Jordan has a love gesture towards his wife, and the emotional distance is broken for a moment. It is understandable that the protagonist starts crying, and her attitude of letting herself be protected, it was the attitude of Jordan what let Alicia show her feelings, which she was holding back because of her husband's character.

Jordan's doctor, on his haste to solve this (yet) unexplainable situation, gives orders that take

Alicia to a vertiginous road to death. When he does not find an explanation for his patient's weakness, his only advice is to rest, and it's precisely resting, lying in bed, that is draining Alicia's life. Of course, we are not suspicious about it, and we even see the doctor's advice as something logical, because he, with his scientific mind, is just trying to ease his patient's pain, even if he does not know the real cause of it.

All the pieces of the puzzle fit when the real cause of Alice's illness is revealed, when the strange animal living in the pillow shows up. Only in the last gasp of the story are the loose ends tied and do we understand the reason for which Alicia's health was getting worse all the time, why the sickness was linked to her blood (she was anemic), and why her life was being drained drop by drop. But as mentioned before, we can see how Quiroga structured the tale in a way in which he plays with our uncertainty and keeps the surprise for the end, achieving his initial purpose.

We also find other two significant parts in this second moment of the narration that deserve to be carefully analyzed. First, there's Jordan's attitude towards his agonizing wife, and second, her hallucinations. In different tales, Horacio Quiroga plays with symbolic elements that somehow refer to death, more specifically, to the ceremonies surrounding it. For instance, he does it in his tale *A la deriva* (*Adrift*), in which it is inferred the walls surrounding the Paraná River enclose him in a way resembling a funeral; we cannot help but see, in this metaphor, the death of Paulino, a death that soon be well accomplished, but at the moment goes on in his death bed adrift. In The feather pillow, the funerary ritual that Jordan is living is totally clear, even if Alicia is still alive. The bedroom where Alicia's body is lying, still living, remains silent and with all its lights on; Jordan visits her and, silently, walks around the room looking at the bed.

The second significant part of the story, besides being very well written, is the one referring to the protagonist's hallucinations. This part, besides showing how the situation gets worse because of Alicia's bad weakness, shows the psychological background in the protagonist's mind, which blooms in the form of a hallucination. It is important to take a look into the content of the hallucinations and, most of all, at how Alicia sees Jordan. There is no doubt that the anthropoid staring at her is nobody but Jordan, and we must ask to ourselves why Alicia has this image of her husband. We know that an anthropoid is an animal with a resemblance to a human, for example, a monkey, but it is not a human, in the end. Now let's take a look at Jordan's character: silent, serious, not very communicative; we understand why Alicia sees her husband this way, it seems that in her altered state of consciousness we see the real image Alicia has of Jordan.

This second moment of the internal structure of the story, the longest one, finishes with the narrator summing up some aspects of Alicia's illness, but also incidentally naming the object that will end up being the center of the attention of this story's end: the pillow.

The last moment, the story's end, begins with the sentence "*Alicia died, eventually*". We said before that the pillow is the center of interest of this third moment of the story, and it is, even to the point that Alicia will not be mentioned in the story ever again. The servant appears, another secondary character (we had already met the doctor), and the only objective of it is to have the reader focus in the pillow. As readers, we give a look to that feather pillow, as the servant does, and the first level of attention stops there, on the object hiding the real cause of the tragedy. Then, there is a dialogue between Jordan and the servant in which the only center of attention is the pillow. The first thing that catches the attention of the servant is a pair of blood spots on the pillow; the second thing is the extraordinary weight of the pillow, which they notice when the servant tries to lift the pillow.

This whole thing unnerves Jordan, and he strikes the pillow with a single blow of a knife, eager to know the truth about the situation, like the origin of the blood spots and the extraordinary weight. Then, the unexpected situation, the ace under the sleeve: the writer shows the terror hiding beneath the feathers, which appears in the last moment to solve all our doubts.

After the description of this strange animal, the narrator gives an explanation about the *Modus operandi* of this creature, how he sucked Alicia's blood and how he had been unnoticed by everyone. Now, with the unexpected appearance of this creature, we tie up all the loose ends of the story and begin to understand each and every pain that Alicia suffered and which ended up killing her.

The last paragraph of the story is very intriguing, it does not feel like it is part of the fiction; instead, it looks more like a scientific explanation about the life and feeding habits of certain parasites that live in birds and sometimes in feather pillows. It seems that Quiroga wants to give a realistic touch to this imaginative display; maybe he did it to try to impress some incautious readers, to make them wonder if the situation could have really happened and wary about the risks involving owning similar pillows.

FELISBERTO HERNÁNDEZ (I)

An author with more advocates than detractors

Felisberto Hernández was an author who inspired as much despise as applauses. Since the first stages of his writing, he received opposed opinions from critics and writers. He received positive and negative reviews regarding to its literature value, criticism that include indifference, rejection and despise, but in the same way, approval, recognition and a very deep admiration.

By: Fernando Chelle

Carlos Maggi, the great Uruguayan writer fromthe "generation of 45", said once: "Felisberto was the main enemy of his literature. He was an insecure guy, shy, like a cornered man. He was desperate for gaining confidence, seeking to be praised or given a favorable opinion" (Di Candia, 2003). It would be good to analyze these words and ponder, from a historical perspective, on why Felisberto was eagerly seeking the approval of his contemporaries.

The "Felisbertian" narrative was a significant break with what had been done so far on in Uruguay. Although Uruguay already had outstanding storytellers within its tradition, such as those of the "900's generation", Javier de Viana with his literature about the countryside and Horacio Quiroga with his stories in urban environments, there was no writer by that moment whose narrative perspective was so associated with the psychological and mental associations, rather than the rational and structured one.

The case of Felisberto is different. His texts have nothing to do with a testimonial realism; His attention to aspects such as the memory, the mystery in everyday life, the relation to the body, the animation of objects, among others, make him an author with an avant-garde look within Uruguayan literature.

Usually, when an author breaks in the artistic field and breaks what is traditionally accepted by critics, the same critics look at him indifferently, marginalize and relegate him. It was kind of what happened to the work of Felisberto Hernández, a certain part of the contemporary critic to the author did not hesitate to attack him.

The Uruguayan critic Alberto Zum Felde, at first, was very hostile to the work of the writer; he did not name him until the third edition of his book *Proceso intelectual de Uruguay* (Intellectual Process of Uruguay). He studied Felisberto from a psychoanalytic point of view of his characters, of whom he says:

"The predominance of sexual complexes is a permanent characteristic in the morbid psychology of his characters, whom the author engages in the fantasy of their circumstances. Almost all of his characters experience libido-related psychosis". (Zum Felde, 1967)

But no doubt, it was Emir Rodriguez Monegal who criticized Felisberto the most, and also analyzed him from a psychoanalytic perspective:

"That child did not grow up anymore. He did not grow up for his life or for his mind, he did not grow up for the art or for sex. He did not grow up for speech. It is true that he is precocious and can touch with his words (after his eyes saw or his hand touched) the instant form of things. (Someone will claim that this is poetry). But he cannot organize his experiences or communicate them; he cannot regulate the fluency of his words. All his immaturity, his absurd precocity, is manifested in that inexhaustible chatter, crossed (sometimes) by some happy expression, but always imprecise, always loose, always overwhelmed with vulgarities, pleonasms, inaccuracies". (Rodríguez Monegal, 1948, pp. 51-52)

Perhaps the use of the first person in the vast majority of the Felisbertian stories, and the fact that he narrates the events that happen to a traveling pianist, caused that a certain part of the critic would not separate, when analyzing it, the reality of a person (the author) and the reality of a fictional character. The author is analyzed as if he were the character, but this is not correct, regardless of whether there are clear similarities between Felisberto and the character of his stories. The artwork belongs to a fictional level, is autonomous and should not analyze a fictional character as if it was the author, because they are different entities.

But while it is true that throughout his life Felisberto received a certain disdain on the part of the critic, also it is certain that he received great compliments and shows of approval to his work.

In 1922, writer, playwright and Felisberto's school teacher José Pedro Bellán, introduced him to the Uruguayan philosopher Carlos Vaz Ferreira, who influenced and positively approved his work. The famous and humble first four Felisberto Hernández's books, known as *Los libros sin tapa* [(*Fulano de tal*, 1925; *Libro sin tapas* (Book without covers), 1929, *La cara de Ana* (The face of Ana), 1930, and *La* envenenada (The poisoned), 1931)] managed to have a positive opinion not only from the philosopher, but also from other writers and intellectuals of his time. Between the people who approved, we can find Antonio Soto, Carlos Mastronardi, Mercedes Pinto and Esther de Cáceres among others.

Regarding the influence of Vaz Ferreira, Norah Giraldi Dei Cas said: "From the philosophical point of view, all of Hernandez's work can be assimilated to some of the fundamental pillars of the so-called 'philosophy of life' in which the thought of Vaz Ferreira is inscribed" (Giraldi Dei Cas, 1975).

On July 31st, 1935, a tribute was paid to Felisberto in the Ateneo Cultural Institute in Montevideo, where the writer Esther de Cáceres, the artist Joaquín Torres García and the literary critic Alberto Zum Felde talked about Felisberto's work.

The support of Joaquín Torres García to the work of Felisberto was also seen in the year 1942 on the occasion of the publication of Felisberto's book, titled *Por los tiempos de Clemente Colling (By the times of Clemente*

Colling). This fundamental book, was the winner of the *Premio Ministerio de Instrucción Pública* (*Ministry of Public Instruction Prize*), which was sponsored by thirteen personalities among whom García was. The following words can be read at the beginning of the book:

"A group of Felisberto Hernandez's friends edit this novel, in recognition of the vast work done by write for this country, and his quality as a composer, concertist and writer." (Hernandez, 1942)

The friends referred are Carmelo de Arzadum, Carlos Benvenuto, Alfredo Cáceres, Spencer Díaz, Luis E. Gil Salguero, Sadí Mesa, José Paladino, Julio Paladino, Yamandú Rodríguez, Clemente Ruggia, Ignacio Soria Gowland, Nicolás Tedesca and Joaquín Torres García.

Around that time, the Uruguayan-French poet Jules Supervielle wrote a consecration letter.

Felisberto added this letter it in the final pages of his book appeared in 1943 *El caballo perdido (The Lost Horse)*

In that letter, Supervielle makes a reference to the impact that caused on him having read *By the times of Clemente Colling*. The letter goes:

"I have had so much pleasure on reading you, on getting to know a really innovative writer who reaches beauty and greatness just by 'being humble in the matters of writing'.

You reach originality without looking for it, just for a natural inclination to intellectual depths. You have an innate sensitivity towards stories that someday will become classics. Your images are always meaningful and fulfill the need of getting engraved in the spirit.

Your narrative contains pages worthy of being featured in rigorous anthologies - they are absolutely admirable - and I congratulate you with all my heart for having given us that book.

Thanks also to your friends who have had the honor of editing those pages.

Yours

Julio Supervielle" (Hernández, 1943)

In addition to supporting, recognizing and spreading Felisberto's work among intellectuals and writers of the time, Supervielle became very important in the life of the Uruguayan storyteller. As Counselor Minister in charge of cultural affairs in the Uruguayan embassy in Paris, in 1946 Felisberto obtains a scholarship granted to him by the French government. The stay of Felisberto in France lasted for two years.

The positive reviews and the praise to the work of Felisberto Hernández happened throughout his life and increased notably after his death.

Just a few days after Felisberto's death, on January 17th, 1964, Angel Rama, a critic who was always a great defender of Felisberto's work, wrote an article titled "On Felisberto Hernández: A gracious poet of matter ", where he says: "One of Uruguay's greatest storytellers, the most original, authentic and talented one, has died "; he also unloaded several criticism against the intellectual environment of the time, which in words of Roberto Ibañez, would only recognize the literary work of Felisberto within twenty years after his death. Rama said in the mentioned article:

"To put it this way, in a controversial tone, or like Ibañez, referring to a possible future recognition, is the same than taking a look to the inertia of this country to perceive art when this art is not born in the agitated and frivolous world of those who believe to own the culture, when it is born outside the conventional society that they have established for

literature, without anyone knowing the origin of this authority or knowledge" (Rama, 1964).

The international recognition from the critics and the readers to the work of Felisberto Hernández came before the time stipulated by Roberto Ibáñez. The year 1974 is very important because his complete works were edited and compiled by José Pedro Díaz; this work had its final edition of three volumes in 1983. On March 31st, 1974, in the city of Buenos Aires, Argentinian writer and journalist Tomás Eloy Martínez wrote an extensive article in La Opinión's cultural supplement titled "*Nobody should forget Felisberto Hernandez*", where he told details of the writer's final stage of his life, and then continued with a complete biography that approached both the Felisberto's personality and some features of his work. Also, in 1974, *Nessuno accendeva le lampade*, the Italian translation of *Nadie encendía las lámparas* (*Nobody would lit the lamps*), was edited by the publishing house Einaudi, from which Italo Calvino highlighted the originality of the Uruguayan storyteller: "*Felisberto Hernández is a writer who looks like no other: he does not look like any of the European nor any of the Latin American writers; he is an 'irregular' who escapes all classification and all framing*". Calvino also states: "...the author has come to conquer a place among the specialists of the Hispanic American fantastic story" (Calvino, 1974).

In 1981, the Ayacucho Library published an edition titled *Felisberto Hernández: Novelas and stories*, in which came a famous letter by Julio Cortázar. In this letter, Argentinian writer expressed his deep admiration and affection for Felisberto Hernández, telling how he was dazzled by tales like *El acomodador (The Usher)* and *Menos Julia (Except for Julia)*, and expresses: "*... I wonder if many of those who ignored or forgave your life then (and still) were not unable to understand why you wrote* *what you wrote and especially why you wrote it like that ...*" (Cortázar, 1981). He described Felisberto as the eleatic of his time for not accepting the logical categories imposed by the tradition and also said that all the wonders and darkness of the world are present in *La casa inundada (The flooded house)*.

There are many and very different writers who both in life and after the death of Felisberto supported his work. There are many more advocates than those referred before, such as the Argentinian poet Oliverio Girondo (who helped Felisberto to publish *Nobody lit the lamps* in the city of Buenos Aires in 1947), Juan Carlos Onetti, Augusto Roa Bastos, Carlos Fuentes (who considered him, along with Juan Carlos Onetti and Horacio Quiroga, an initiator of the new Latin American literature). We could also add the names of other artists who commented positively the Felisbertian work. According to Walter Rela, Felisberto "*had comments on letters that he proudly showed, coming from Amado Alonso, Gomez de la Serna, Mallea, Puccini, Mastronardi*" (Rela, 2002)

In 2002, a tribute was paid to Felisberto Hernández at the Autonomous University of Mexico, on commemoration of the centenary of his birth. It began with a telegram from the Colombian Nobel Prize winner Gabriel García Márquez in which he recognized that if he had not read Felisberto, he would never have become the writer that he was.

References

Calvino, Italo. Prólogo a *Nessuno accendeva le lampade*, Turín, Einaudi, 1974.

Cortázar, Julio. *Carta a mano propia*, en *Felisberto Hernández: Novelas y cuentos*, Caracas, Biblioteca Ayacucho, 1981.

Di Candia, Cesar. Homenaje a la Generación del 45 y a sus antecesores: Felisberto, Onetti, Paco [Quoted in *El País Digital* de 31 mayo 2003].

Giraldi Dei Cas, Norah. *Felisberto Hernández, del creador al hombre*, Montevideo, Ediciones de la Banda Oriental, 1975.

Hernández, Felisberto. *Por los tiempos de Clemente Colling*, Montevideo, González Panizza Hnos. Editores, 1942.

Hernández, Felisberto. *El caballo perdido*, Montevideo, González Panizza Hnos. Editores, 1943.

Rama, Ángel. Sobre Felisberto Hernández: Burlón poeta de la materia, Semanario *Marcha*, Montevideo, January 1964 [in *El País Cultural* de December 31st 1993].

Rela, Walter. Felisberto Hernández, Persona – Obra, Cronología documentada, Homenaje en el centenario del nacimiento, Biblioteca Nacional, 2002.

Rodríguez Monegal, Emir. "*Nadie encendía las lámparas*", Revista Clinamen, Montevideo: Año II, N° 5, mayo / junio 1948, pp. 51-52. Quoted by Claudio Paolini en Felisberto Hernández: Escritor maldito o poeta de la materia [en 2003].

Zum Felde, Alberto. *Proceso intelectual del Uruguay* (Tomo III), Montevideo, Nuevo Mundo, 1967.

[1] About Julio Cortázar: Centenario del nacimiento de Julio Cortázar. Continuidad de los parques (lectura comentada), by Fernando Chelle, in the previous issue of ***vadenuevo***

[2] El presente artículo continuará en la próxima edición de ***vadenuevo*** con un abordaje específico de algunos aspectos de la obra del narrador uruguayo y el análisis literario de alguno de sus cuentos. This article will be continued in the next issue of ***vadenuevo*** and will be focused in some aspects of the uruguayan writer's work, as well as the analysis of one of his stories.

FELISBERTO HERNÁNDEZ (II)

The fantastic strangeness of daily life

An original, unstructured, self-fictional, strange, highly humoristic narrator. A writer who writes like no other: the fantastic Felisberto. In this article: stages and characteristics of his work, along with a literary analysis of his short story *Muebles: el canario (The canary: furniture shop)*.

By: Fernando Chelle

In the last issue of **Vadenuevo** magazine, we found the first part of a study on the works of the Uruguayan writer Felisberto Hernández. The objective of the mentioned article was to analyze the reception of Hernandez's works among literary critics and writers through history. In this article, you will find an analysis on the different stages of his works and its main characteristics, as well as an analysis to one of his most famous stories: *The Canary: furniture shop.*

The literary works of Felisberto Hernandez can be divided in three stages:

a) Initiation, from his first four books: *Fulano de tal* (1925), *Libro sin tapas* (1929), *La cara de Ana* (1930) and *La envenenada* (1931)

b) Maturity, a stage that includes *Por los tiempos de Clemente Colling* (1942) and *El caballo perdido* (1943)

c) Final stage, which includes the rest of his works: *Tierras de la memoria* (published after his death in 1965), *Nadie encendía las lámparas* (1947), *Las hortensias* (1949) y *La casa inundada (*1960).

To this classification in stages, we must add other works and fragments that belong to other periods which were published in a posthumous way, in *Diario del sinvergüenza (Diary of a shameless man*) and *Últimas invenciones* (*Last inventions* published by Editorial Arca in 1974. In a different publication by Editorial Arca in 1969 titled *Primeras invenciones (First inventions*), we can find, besides his first four books, four unpublished short stories, and other short stories published in newspapers, as well as three poems from the years 1932 and 1934. Felisberto had an incursion in the lyric genre, as well as in the drama, he wrote a short plays, but Felisberto did not keep working those genres.

Characteristics of the work of Felisberto Hernández

The first thing we notice when we face any of Felisberto's works is the fact that we are in front of an original narrator, whom stories do not follow the traditional tracks of narrative organization. His stories seem to lack a solid structure to hold them, they are built through the association of ideas and motivations, and most of them do not have a concluding end. The internal atmospheres of his tales are strange, the objects seem to have a life of their own, the parts of the bodies seem to be independent, reality meets fantasy, and everything is expressed with a simple and colloquial language with big doses of humor.

In his stories, we can also remark the repetition of the topics or motivations, specifically, the events that occur to a traveling pianist. It is very important to note that the narrative material worked by Felisberto was mostly taken from real life. In most of his stories, we can say there is a very strong self-biographic component, because Felisberto was a traveling pianist himself, who roamed around small cities inside Uruguay and Argentina playing concerts. Hernandez found a way to use his reality as a source of inspiration for his literature. He took historical elements and turned them into literary elements from a retrospective view where the memories play a key role. The memories of those little cities and towns, with their humble theaters, trading places and parks, can be found in his tales. You will never find a precise identification of a determined place; for example, the action in stories as *El balcón* (*The balcony*) and *El cocodrilo* (*The crocodile*), might as well happen in Rocha or in Florida, as well as Mercedes, just to name three similar cities to those in which Felisberto published his first works. Maybe, the easiest place to identify can be found in *Por los tiempos de Clemente Colling,* where the manors of the zone of El Prado in Montevideo and the route of the 42nd tramway are recreated, but even this determined place works in function of the evocation, and does not answer the need to recreate geographical or historical aspects, because the interest point of this story are the character's memories.

This notorious self-biographic component in Felisberto's works can be named self-fiction; it's linked directly to the style the author decided to give his stories. We only can see a third person narrator in a few of these stories, the vast majority of his stories are told using a first person narrator. This characteristic gives his stories a sober, colloquial, informal tone. Felisberto did the transmutation of the historical elements into literary elements with total simplicity, using everyday words, direct and easy to understand, leaving aside the more complex and rhetorical ones. This conversational style, not typical of the academic circle, was one of the main targets where the critics attacked his works, accusing him of having a limited vocabulary. Maybe these critics, used to their own stylistic parameters, were not able to appreciate the use of an adequate vocabulary for the tone of Felisberto's stories, characters and situations, which gives the reader a clear feeling of naturalness and spontaneity.

Linked to the first person voice, the narrated stories always refer to the narrator's own time: Just the same way it happens with space, the time in the felisbertian narrations is typically undetermined. We know, for the use of certain grammar tenses that the foretold stories happened in the past. Some stories refer to facts, places and characters that Felisberto seems to have taken from his childhood and others from his mature age, but in the regular evocations in his stories, the time seems to dilute, and the events in his stories are just events that happened before the moment of the narration.

One of the most noticeable characteristics in the literature of Felisberto is a small dose of humor. Humor, comedy, as Calvino said *"transfigures the bitterness of a life knit of defeats"*. Humor, in the works of Felisberto, allows absurdity of certain situations, dissolving events that otherwise might be considered distressful or painful if they were given a different literary treatment. Vital situations, as those faced by the protagonists in *The crocodile* or *The canary: furniture shop,* are not humoristic per se, they are quite the opposite. Humor becomes the vehicle that allows transit in a path of confusion and discomfort.

Another particular characteristic in Felisberto's narrative is the treatment given to objects and the parts of the body. In *By the times of Clemente Colling,* the narrator character says *"During that time, my attention stopped in those things in the background"*. This implies a different look on things, where he tries to unravel its mysteries, its secret and unexplainable functionality from a rational point of view. In these stories, objects seem to have their own life, to have a persona, and are not just there for the utilitarian use that mankind gives them.

Something similar, but in an inverse way, happens to the parts of the body, which are treated like mere objects. There is a not so common look on the human body, and its parts seem to be autonomous objects with a life of their own. We can perceive this in many stories, but this perk is more noticeable in *Diary of a shameless man* where the narrator has a dialogue with his own body. We can see how this felisbertian world establishes a very strange link between unanimated things and living beings turned into objects.

FANTASY

To put it very briefly, we say fantastic literature are those stories that show events that the reader cannot explain recurring to interpretations that start from a possible reality. The fantastic story shows the reader some strange, surprising event in the midst of circumstances that can be called normal. Facing this, the reader may feel doubts, uncertainty and surprise, but he must accept what is being told possible in the fiction, even if these events are unexplainable from a rational point of view.

There has been a lot of discussion by critics and writers about including or not the literature of Felisberto Hernández within the fantastic genre. Some of them do not hesitate to call it fantastic; others accept the qualification, but with certain restrictions, and there are those who definitely refuse to place him within this category. I believe that the problem here lies in the traditional eagerness, not only by critics, of wanting to match works of art to models, schools or canonical tendencies. This classificatory intention can be very useful in establishing similarities and differences between certain artistic manifestations, but we must understand that works are independent expression of certain molds. Apart from this, we cannot refer to the whole of Hernandez's work as belonging or not to the fantastic genre; there are some stories that undoubtedly have the characteristics that critics like Todorov attribute to the fantastic genre and we also find other stories that definitely cannot be classified into this genre.

In a great number of his stories, Felisberto Hernández gives way to fantasy in the middle of situations that can be described as normal, real, plausible. Fantasy, in some of these narrations, is created with the same elements that make up the real world, which is approached in a different way. Felisberto generally introduces strangeness and fantasy in his texts using expressions or linguistic twists, for example: "*In that moment many things happened*", "*It happened that ...*" , without it being a relationship of cause and effect between what was happening in the narration and what is going to happen next.

LITERARY ANALYSIS

The text chosen for a literary analysis is *The Canary, Furniture Shop*, a text included in the book *Nobody lit the lamps*, published by Editorial Sudamericana in Buenos Aires in 1947.

The central topic of the story is the media invasion in favor of advertising, and the way it affects the privacy.

When I wrote about the characteristics of Felisberto's works, I said that his stories do not follow the traditional narrative organization; I also said that his stories lack of a solid structure holding on them, and they are built through the association of ideas and motivations that, in the end, do not show a concluding ending. This is exactly what happens in *The canary, Furniture Shop*. When we analyze this work trying to determine his internal structure, we face the difficulty implied in separating unerringly the different moments that form the story. Anyway, in this short story we can appreciate a succession of chained events that are shown in a non-fluent way, and I will try to show the links of that chain.

The first moment of the story happens when the main character of the story is coming back to his city and becomes the victim of an unusual, surprising and weird event, as he gets a substance injected in his arm without his consent. We can determine a second moment (remember this is just for analysis purposes), and which begins when the character gets down the streetcar: the inner thoughts of the protagonist become the center of interest of this segment, the reflections about what just happened and the beginning of the weird and fantastic events that he suffered. The third part of the story is marked by the protagonist's efforts to nullify the effects of the injection inoculated to him; finally, the fourth and last segment of the story consists on the ending, in which the protagonist dialogues with a man who is injecting some kids.

The advertisement of this furniture company got me unaware. I was on a one month vacation in a nearby place and did not want to know what was happening in the city. When I arrived back, the weather was hot, and that same night I went to the beach. I was heading back to my room, and I was a bit upset for what had happened in the streetcar. I got on it at the beach and had to sit in one of the hallway's seats. As the weather was still very hot, I had my coat on my knees and my arms were receiving the air, because I was wearing a short sleeved shirt.

The beginning of the story is abrupt. There is no introduction to place the character in a specific time or place before the action; we only have the words of the protagonist narrator. The first sentence of the story is very important, because it tells two things: on one side, the main theme of the story, "advertisement", on the other hand, the attitude of the guy towards this advertisement, because the protagonist says "*The advertisement (...) got me unaware*", at which we might understand that there is a way to be aware of the siege of the advertisement. We may find in this segment an implicit criticism towards the invasion of the media in the service of advertisement. The main character's will was not to know in this city because he was on vacation in a nearby place; here we can appreciate, as I had told before, that there is not a precise identification of the places where actions take place: the place where he was on holiday was just a nearby place.

If we take a look to the use of the tenses, we can appreciate that this homodiegetic narrator is talking from the future. "*The advertisement of this furniture company got me unaware*". This is another Felisberto's characteristic we had already pointed: the story he is telling belongs to the past, already happened.

The main character says he went back to his "room", not his house, and this is very meaningful; remember when we talked about the strong self-biographical element in the works of Felisberto. Well, as a traveling pianist, he used to sleep in rooms of small hotels, which names are often referenced throughout his works; this seems to be one of those cases. But let's take look on what happened in the streetcar: the main character sits in one of the hallway seats, with his coat on his knees and his arms in the air; the writer prepares the terrain for the events about to happen.

Among the people around the hallway, there was one person who suddenly said to me:

-Excuse me, please…

And I quickly answered him:

-Take it.

But not only hadn't I understood what was going on, I also got afraid. Many things happened in that moment. First on of them was, even before he had not finished asking for my permission yet, before I had finished answering him, he was rubbing my naked arm with something cold that I, I do not know why, thought was saliva. And when I just had finished saying "It's yours", I felt the sting and saw a big syringe with some letters. At the same time, a fat lady in a different seat said:

- Go ahead

I must have done an abrupt movement with my arm because the man with the needle said:

-Eh, I'll end up hurting you… just hold on…

He was soon handling the syringe while the other passengers who had seen my face were laughing. Then he began to rub the arm of the fat lady while she looked at the operation with complacency. Despite the needle was big, it could throw just a small squirt with a spring stroke. Then I was able to read the yellow letters along the tube: "The canary, Furniture Company". I was too embarrassed to ask what was it about and I decided I would know the next day by the newspapers.

There is a dialogue between the man who injects the passengers and the protagonist, and we, as readers, become some kind of standing witness of the scene going on. When the protagonist says "*go ahead*", he is not allowing the man to inject him; the protagonist probably thought that the man was asking him for a space so he could pass to a seat: he ignores these new advertisement strategies. With the sentence "*Many things happened in that moment*", Felisberto begins to tell the absurd events that lead to fantasy.

There is a contrast between the attitude of the protagonist and the attitude of the other passengers, which seem to know beforehand the advertising methods used by companies; on the other hand, the protagonist feels baffled, astonished and scared by the events. Let's take a look at the different attitudes: for example, the protagonist makes a sudden movement with his arm, in total ignorance of what is going on, even taking the risk of getting hurt, while the fat woman, knowing the methodology, watched the operation with a pleasant look. The fat woman's attitude towards the facts is comical, but it is precisely that humorous treatment that Felisberto gives to the story which allows him to continue to tell about an absurd situation as if it were something normal.

If we wanted to give the story a symbolic reading, we could see the tram as a representation of society and its behavior towards the arrival of a consuming society, marked by the omnipresence of different forms of advertising. In that reading, the protagonist is the exception, a stranger in the middle of smiling and alienated passengers adjusted to the social parameters. The fact of being the exception, apparently the only one who does not understand the situation, leads the character to feel ashamed, instead of encouraging him to ask what is it all about.

But as soon as I got off of the tram I thought: "It won't be a strengthener, this must be something that leaves visible consequences, if it is really an advertisement". However, I did not know for sure what it was about; but I was too tired and I became obstinate about not thinking about it. Anyway, I was sure that to doping people with any drug was not allowed by law. Before falling asleep, I thought that, in the best of cases, they had wanted to produce a feeling of wellbeing or pleasure. I was still awake when I began to hear inside of me, the tweets of a little bird. It did not have the quality of a remembered sound, neither the sound that comes from the outside. It was not normal, like some brad new sickness, but it had an ironic hue, as if the sickness was feeling happy and would have started to sing.

When I mentioned fantastic literature, I said that it shows a fantastic happening to the reader, a strange event, surprising, amidst circumstances that can be called "normal"; you just have to take a look to the events that the main character suffers, without any explanation, to classify this story in this genre.

Even if the protagonist is not among the general alienation of the people inside the tram, the social parameters do not cease conditioning him, because he is ashamed of being different anyway, of dissenting with the majority of the people; and, instead having a somehow precise reaction, he waits until he has got off of the bus to make hypothesis, some of them supernatural about what just happened. Having read the words *The canary, furniture shop* in the syringe is what makes the protagonist suppose that it is some kind of advertisement, but he cannot conceive that an advertisement does not leave visible marks; he will soon begin to feel the real consequences of this injection. The sentence *"Anyway, I was sure that it was not allowed to dope the people with any drug"* is very meaningful to me, because it is loaded with irony. Because, we must ask to ourselves ¿What are the limits for the advertisement invasion in a consumer society? ¿What do drugs generate and what does consumerism generate once advertisement has invaded the mind of the consumers? Both things generate a necessity, a desire, and finally a dependency. Both things are used sometimes by the individuals to fill gaps and getting temporary pleasure.

The fantastic event begins just the moment before the main character falls asleep, when he begins to hear the tweet of a bird inside of his head. This event is deeply strange, but we as readers must accept what we are being told as possible inside this narrative fiction, even if it appears to be an unexplainable event, from a rationalist point of view. The character states that the bird's tweet is some kind of *"brand new sickness"*, and immediately after, Felisberto relies in one of his favorite artifices: the animation of concepts or objects. Even the feelings have an independent life of their own. In this particular case, the sickness suffered by the protagonist feels happy and begins to sing.

This particular aspect, besides giving the sickness a life of its own, has a very oxymoronic, contradictory feeling, because sickness is the last element related to joy.

These sensations passed quickly and immediately appeared something more concrete: I heard a voice in my head that said:

Hey ho, this is "The canary" broadcasting… hey ho, special audition. People sensitized for this broadcastings… etc, etc.

I was hearing all of this standing on my feet, barefoot, aside my bed and not daring to turn the lights on; I had jumped and stood still in that place. It seemed impossible that it sounded inside my head. I went back to my bed and decided to wait. Now they were broadcasting indications about the payment in monthly fees in the furniture shop "The canary". And then they suddenly said:

As a first issue, we will broadcast a tango titled…

After the tweet of the little bird comes a sound that the protagonist considers "*more concrete*": it is a human voice, a radio announcer who, sounds inside his head as the bird tweets. The protagonist leaves aside the narrative voice and reproduces what the radio announcer is saying, leaving the protagonist in the role of the listener. It is a radio broadcast, and the name of the radio station has by chance the same name that the needle in the tram had: "The canary". The radio announcer is talking about a special audition, referencing people who have been sensitized to listen to the aforementioned broadcasts, the injected ones. Later, the narrator makes a description of himself, where he declares himself scared, *"not daring to turn the lights on"*, baffled, without believing what was happening. We learned, and now again by the voice of the character, that the radio is an advertising tool at the service of the furniture shop "The canary" where they announce the benefits that customers have, such as the possibility of paying the furniture in monthly fees. The voice of the announcer appears again to announce the first musical number of the broadcast; it is "the tango", which will take the character to the ultimate desperation. There is a punctual fact here that shows the dislike that the protagonist feels for the tango; the voice of the announcer does not even specify a particular tango, but simply says "tango", which would show that rejection includes all musical manifestations of that musical genre. As I said before, the works of Felisberto Hernández are so strongly influenced by the author's own life that I did a research about his views on tango, but did not find any information about that specific topic. Anyway, there is one important fact: in the year of 1943, one of his jobs in the *Asociación de Radio Uruguaya de Autores* (Uruguayan Author's Radio Association) was to listen radio during entire hours, writing on a paper the songs that had been played, so the author's association could manage the payment of the copyright. Probably, many of the broadcasted songs were tangos, I do not know, but surely, doing that almost Kafkaesque job ended up with him hating radio and advertisement.

Exasperated, I got under a thick blanket; then I heard everything more clearly, for the blanket attenuated the noise of the street and I perceived better what was happening inside my head. Immediately I took off the blanket and began to walk around the room; this relieved me a little but I had something like a secret stubbornness in hearing and complaining about my misfortune. I went to bed again and when I grabbed the bars of the bed, I heard the tango more clearly.

The desperation for escaping away of the tango is what makes the character go under the blanket, but it happens that he cannot escape. It is an internal noise, and the only thing he achieves is hearing the sounds inside his head more clearly. When he is under the blanket, he is totally isolated from the surrounding world, and linked exclusively to the radio station and the broadcast and the media manipulation. Desperation can be noticed in the constant change of moods of the main character: he does not know if he should stay under the blanket, leave his bed, walk the room or go back to bed. There is a paradoxical situation: even if the character is suffering having to hear the broadcasts, he wants to hear it and complain about his misfortune. There is also an absurd-humoristic situation, when the main character grabs the bars of the bed: everything makes the readers suppose that the bars were made of metal, because they cause that the tango is heard more clearly because they work as some kind of antenna.

After a while I found myself in the street again: I was looking for other noises that attenuated the one that I was hearing inside my head. I thought about buying a newspaper to inform myself about the radio station address to ask them what I had to do to nullify the effect of the injection. But a tram came and I took it. In a few moments the tram passed by a place where the tracks were in poor condition and the big noise relieved me of another tango they were playing now; But suddenly I looked into the streetcar and saw another man with another syringe; he was injecting children who were sitting in crossed seats. I went there and asked him what I had to do to cancel the effect of an injection they applied on me an hour ago.

Audition keeps disturbing the character who now, in desperation, decides to leave his house looking for a solution. His discomfort is so bad that he feels he is just looking for other noises to attenuate the internal noise that is giving him a bad time. Just as he thought while being on the tram, he wants to look for information on the newspapers, but now he does not intend to make clear what the injection is all about, because he totally knows it for sure now: he wants to find the address of the radio station, as all he thinks about in this moment is in how to nullify the effect of this annoying injection. Desperation leads him to abandon that idea too, and to take a tram again. For a moment, temporarily, he achieved the goal he had set out on the street: to soften his head with other noises, since *"the tram passed through a place where the roads were in poor condition and the great Noise relieved me of another tango they played now* " Getting on the tram ends up being beneficial, since there he meets another employee of this large multidisciplinary corporation called "*The canary*", which is injecting children, and from which he will obtain first-hand information. As we can see, advertisement doses are not restricted to a certain age group and even the most socially vulnerable are "sensitized" through this perverse methodology.

He looked at me with and expression of surpire and said:

- Don't you like the broadcast?

- Not at all

- Just wait for a moment, a radio novel should begin soon

-Awful –I said.

He kept injecting and shaking his head, forming a smile. I did not hear the tango anymore. Now they were talking again about furniture. At last, the man with the syringe told me:

-Sir, the advertisement of the pills "The canary" has appeared in every newspaper. If you don't like the broadcast, you just take one of them, and that's it.

-But all the drugstores are closed right now, and I'm going mad!

In that moment, I head an announcement:

-And now we will hear a poem called "My dear couch", a sonnet written specially for the furniture shop "The canary".

After that, the man with the syringe approached me to talk to my ears and said:

-I'm going to fix your problem in a different way. I'll charge you one peso because I see the face of an honest man in yours. If you tell anybody about this, I'd lose my job, for it's better for the company that the pills are sold.

I hurried him to tell me the secret. Then he opened his hand and said:

-Bring on the peso

And I gave it to him and he added:

-Wash your feet on hot water.

And here we reach the outcome of the story, where the predominant element is the protagonist narrator and the The Canary's worker. The situation faced by these two characters can be compared to the one we witnessed on the first tram, where the other passengers were smiling because of the ignorance of the main character. Here, this worker smiles and is thrilled to find someone who not only seems to be outside the consumption society, but also wants to get rid of it. The worker seems amazed of how little informed is this character, because the solution to his problems is in every newspaper. To end the broadcastings of "*Broadcast station: The Canary*", where the "*Furniture shop: The Canary*" advertises its products, people must take pills named "*The Canary*". This monopolist trademark produces the illness and also the cure, and with that marketing methodology, if the company does not sell the furniture, at least will get a certain profit from selling the pills calmly, because the ordinary people seems to be pleased and satisfied with this kind of services. Undoubtedly, there is a strong criticism implicit in this story, not only against the media, but also against consumption society. For us, 21st century readers, it is nothing new to see a certain trademark trying to monopolize certain products or services, but almost 70 years ago, when this short story was written, this situation was very unlikely to happen.

The character cannot afford the situation anymore. He even thinks that he is going crazy with such bombing of advertisement, novels in episodes, tangos and silly, ridiculous poetry. At the end of the story, in a very ironic way, the worker gives the protagonist an alternative solution to his suffering. Irony can be seen in the fact that the employee of The Canary talks about honesty at the same time that he trespasses his functions. On the other hand, he is not doing any favor or solidary action; instead, he is taking advantage of the protagonist's despair for his own benefit. Once the character accepts the fraudulent transaction for the agreed fee, the words of the worker that contain the cure, the solution, the ultimate exit to his calm: *"Wash your feet on hot water."*

It is a typical feature on felisbertian stories: the ending is not conclusive and seems abrupt. We don't know which of the possible options the main character is going to choose to end his misery, if he will fall on the trap of the monopoly built by *The canary* buying the pills or if he will choose the hot wash.

As a conclusion: *The canary, furniture shop* is a fantastic short story, completely anchored in a recognizable reality, which allows us to enjoy, feel and live the story. The topic has an amazing validity. Nowadays, more than ever, we should be prevented of the advertisement and propagandistic attacks, maybe in a different way than the protagonist suffered, but in an omnipresent way in our daily lives. Business monopolies are not new for us, 21st century readers, and neither are visual and noise pollution in our daily spaces. Advertisement is not exclusive from the TV, radio, newspapers, magazines or spam mails, it can also be found on the street, on the street corners, delivered by promoters, in the mailboxes of the buildings, in the cinemas, in the shopping malls and basically any place where there are potential consumers. Sad thing is, our reality lacks of these kinds of solution that are present in the fiction, and these problems are not solved with a hot water feet wash.

JORGE LUIS BORGES

The Aleph. The infinite multiplicity of the universe

With excerpts of the translation by Norman Thomas Di Giovanni in collaboration with Borges, MIT

A look into a paradigmatic short story by Jorge Luis Borges. Many literary critics consider this story one of the best fiction works in the whole 20th century.

By: Fernando Chelle

The text chosen for analysis in this literary article belongs to Argentinian writer Jorge Luis Borges (Buenos Aires, Argentina, August 24^{th,} 1899 – Ginebra, Switzerland, June 14^{th,} 1986). It is a short story named *El Aleph* (*The*

Aleph), considered one of the best fiction works in the 20th century by a part of the whole world's literary critics. The story was first published in the *Revista Sur (Sur Magazine)* in the year of 1945, and was later part of a homonymous book published by *Editorial Emecé* in Buenos Aires in 1949.

This paradigmatic short story is the final one in a book that contains seventeen stories; each one of them, in their own way, are about a particular set of things (about some catalogue), and every story has the most recurrent topics of the Argentinian writer; time, death, the search for knowledge linked with curiosity, kabbalah, labyrinths, libraries, references to different universally canonic literary works, the inability of mankind to face the eternity, the universe, gods, luck. The story takes the name of the mathematic symbol $\aleph$ (Aleph number) the number that symbolizes the size of infinite sets, and represents the infiniteness of the universe, according to the cabalistic mystical doctrines. Mystical Jews see the first letter of the Hebrew alphabet as the spiritual root of all the letters, a letter that contains all the others, thus containing all the elements of the human language. According to this tradition, the letter א (ɑːlɛf) is a symbol of the universe and God's will, as it was the only letter that mortals heard directly from the voice of God.

This book, where tradition and metaphysics converge, is written in a sober, understandable way, despite its deep prose. It has the virtue of approaching very complex topics in simple plots, which can be seen clearly in this story. Even if it recreates a transcendental experience, the narration is simple, linear.

The story is narrated in first person by a narrator protagonist, who has the same last name of the author; this is nothing but a game played by the author that helps to blur the parameters that separate reality and fiction, added to other elements with a believable nature that recreate a recognizable reality.

The main plot is the protagonist facing the infinite, represented in an object called the Aleph, which is nothing but a point in the universe (micro cosmos) which contains all the points of the universe. Borges-writer has used a procedure that consists in locating an object of symbolic characteristics in a real, daily life environment, a basement in the city of Buenos Aires. Fantasy is characterized in the inclusion a supernatural object on a daily life environment; in the case of this story, there are totally realistic features anchored in a perfectly believable and recognizable reality. There, not only the city of Buenos Aires can be found, the neighborhood Constitución is present too, as well as the names of writers like Juan Crisóstomo Lafinur and Pedro Enríquez Ureña, among other references of the real world; this allows Borges to play with a believable reality, turn it into a fiction and then go deep into another fantastic dimension where the Aleph can be found.

While describing the multiplicity of the things in the universe seen in the Aleph, narrator faces the impossibility of doing it effectively, using such a limited resource as language; that is the reason behind the use of chaotic numerations that somehow try to express an unending succession. But even if this is the main topic of the story, there are other two topics that also take part of the narrative axis. Those are: the frustrated love between Borges-protagonist and late Beatriz Viterbo; on the other hand, the personal relationship between Borges-protagonist with Beatriz's cousin, Carlos Argentino Daneri.

The story can be divided in three stages: first, the happenings in the life of the protagonist before the contemplation of the Aleph, then the beholding of the object, and finally, the reflections of the protagonist on the contemplation of the wonderful element.

After two brief quotes, one from Shakespare and another from *Leviathan*, the short-story starts telling about the death of Beatriz Viterbo, a friend to the protagonist-narrator. The first part of the story tells the happenings on Borges-protagonist before beholding the Aleph and how he became a frequent visitor of the house of his dead friend, in that place he meets Beatriz's father, and mainly her cousin, Carlos Argentino Daneri, author of a poem called *"La tierra"* (The earth), in which he tries to express the roundness of the planet. Borges, the character, has extensive talks with Daneri, something that Borges-writer uses to express his points of view on different concepts about literature. Borges-writer has created a satirical character, Daneri, who personifies the image of a pseudo-poet awarded with international prizes; it is undoubtedly an implicit critic towards bad literature from Borges-author. The paragraphs written by Beatriz's cousin, considered valuable by their author, are nothing but clumsy, extravagant versifications. In one occasion, Daneri phone calls Borges to invite him to drink milk in a Bar, property of Zunino and Zungri, the owners of the house in Garay street where he had traditionally lived. There, Daneri reads some lines of his poems for Borges, who is afraid that the author will ask him to write the prologue for his book, something that won't happen, because Daneri's true intention for Borges is that he works as an intermediary between him and Álvaro Melián Lafinur, so it is this last mentioned person the one who will be tasked to prologue the book. At first, Borges accepts to be the intermediary and talk to Lafinur, but once he leaves Carlos Argentino Daneri, thinks about it and decides not to do it, and take responsibility for his own decision. Some months later, Borges receives another phone call by Daneri, who in desperation, tells him that Zunino and Zungri are planning to demolish the house in Garay street where, Daneri confesses Borges, there is a basement that has an Aleph, a space where all the spaces of the orb meet, that he had discovered it while he was a kid and was necessary to him to finish a novel that he was writing. After hearing these words, Borges feels tempted to go immediately to meet the wonderful object. Once at Daneri's home, the host offers Borges a cup of cognac, invites him to go to the basement and indicates him the position he must adopt in order to behold the Aleph. For a while, Borges suspects that Daneri is planning to kill him, and that his own curiosity led him to the trap, but nothing of this happens. After following the steps given by Daneri in order to see the object, he can finally contemplate the universe in a precise point. The amazed protagonist sees a sphere which center is everywhere and its circumference is nowhere; an object where Everything is reflected, where the space has no limits and where the time is all the times fused in a simultaneous reality; he sees several places from different places, he sees the past, the present and the future, and accesses the universe's best hidden secrets. The fantastic contemplation makes the protagonist feel wonder and pity, and only thing he can say to Daneri, who looks for the complicity of his guest is *"One hell of a... Yes, one hell of a..."*[1] Borges decides not to talk with his host about the magnificent vision and urges him to make profit of the demolition taking distance once and for all from the Aleph. Borges decides not to answer the question Daneri makes to him: *"Did you see everything – really clear, in colors?"*

---

[1] In its original language, a more accurate translation would be "Fantastic, indeed, fantastic", but Norman Di Giovanni's translation, one of the most popular on the internet, goes "One hell of a..."; this is translation is particularly valuable as was done in collaboration with Borges himself.

The short story ends with a postscript where the protagonist informs that the house was finally demolished in 1943 and therefore the Aleph was destroyed. It also refers to the fate of Daneri as a writer and to two circumstances about the nature of the Aleph, one about its origin and another about the possibility of it being fake. These reflections are based on quotes from some texts of classic and contemporary authors. Another hypothesis about what happened to the object comes when the protagonist tells about the possibility of having seen the object, but also having forgotten about it after that.

We can establish an undeniable parallelism between this story and certain parts of works such as Dante's *Inferno,* as we can compare Beatriz Viterbo to Beatriz Portinari, because it is thanks to her that Borges – as well as Dante – can reach divinity, represented in this case by the Aleph. Something similar happens with Plato's *"The republic"*, where we can compare the descent to the basement to the myth of the cavern, where characters are motionless and watching images that substitute the reality. But these parallelisms, as well as the possible interpretations we can make about this short story from different points of view, literary, philosophical, theological, etc. would make part of a study that exceeds the length of this one, in which I just tried to approach an essential text of the literature of the past century.

JULIO CORTÁZAR

"Continuity of the parks" (Commented Reading)

In this short story, we can find the main characteristics that make the writer of *Rayuela* (Hopscotch) one of the greatest masters of Latin-American and world literature

With excerpts of the translation hosted in
http://www.utdallas.edu/~aargyros/continuity_of_the_parks.ht
m

By: Fernando Chelle

There are many literary aspects that we can analyze when we approach Julio Cortázar. We can analyze his importance as a novelist and the relevance of his novel for the Latin-American literature, or his social essays, and even his work as a teacher. But this time, I will address a story that came out in 1964 and is part of the second edition of the book *Final del juego* (*End of the game*), edited by Editorial Sudamericana; It's an analysis on the story *Continuidad de los parques* (*Continuity of the parks*).

I chose this short story mainly because we can find there the main features that make the writer of *Hopscotch* one of the greatest masters of Latin American and world literature. In the few lines of the story, we meet the short-story master, the author who broke the molds, canons and stereotypes of the mainstream literature of his time, there is also a time and speech transgression, as well as an exquisite breakpoint between reality and fantasy.

The main topic of this short story is the continuity established between two fiction worlds. The first world, which we will call primary fiction, is the reality of a man who is reading a novel; the first world ends up linked to a second fictional world, the world of the characters of the novel the man is reading. The places where the two worlds meet are precisely, the parks, the park of the novel reader (primary fiction), and the park of the woods in the lover's cabin (secondary fiction), that end up melting, fusing, continuing. As we can see, the title of the short story is present in the main topic of it.

Regarding the external or formal structure of the story, we can see it is divided in two paragraphs that somehow correspond to their thematic content. Even if there are three moments in the narration, the first two come together in the first paragraph, and the last moment comes in its totality in the last paragraph.

The first moment of the story focuses on what I called primary fiction and brings the presentation of the reading man and the world surrounding him. Among this first big paragraph, we also find the second moment, which I called secondary fiction. And which point of interest are the events of the novel that the reader character is reading. Finally, in the third moment, which we can find in the third paragraph, we meet the fantastic element of the story, the fusion of both fictions.

> *He had begun to read the novel a few days before. He had put it aside because of some urgent business conferences, opened it again on his way back to the estate by train; he permitted himself a slowly growing interest in the plot, in the characterizations.*

That afternoon, after writing a letter giving his power of attorney and discussing a matter of joint ownership with the manager of his estate, he returned to the book in the tranquility of his study which looked out upon the park with its oaks. (Cortázar, 1964)

The intention of the author of the story is raised from the beginning; his interest is that we focus in those aspects that make the central idea of the story, the fusion of two fictional worlds. That's why he chooses not to give us physical or psychological information on the reader character, as they are meaningless for the plot of the story. Only thing that matters is how the character works on the story. Nevertheless, the omniscient narrator gives certain information about the life of the reader, but this information will be at the plot's service. In the first stage of the story, in short, both fictions are already approached: the reader and the novel. The main thing here is to quickly focus on the importance that the novel will end up having for its reader. References about urgent businesses, about his attorney and his butler are working in two ways: showing the state of wealth and welfare of the reader character and, on the other side, how this protagonist finished all his chores in order to sit and read peacefully. For the events that are going to arise in the story, it was necessary that the reading character was totally relaxed, so the fiction he was reading would absorb him totally. Tranquility offered by his studio, whose window had a view to the oak's park, makes the perfect place to let the character go inside the plot of the novel.

> *Sprawled in his favorite armchair, its back toward the door--even the possibility of an intrusion would have irritated him, had he thought of it--he let his left hand caress repeatedly the green velvet upholstery and set to*

reading the final chapters. (Cortázar, 1964)

In this brief but convincing narration, all the elements that appear are an important part of the story; they are not there just for decoration. Logically Cortázar knew perfectly the way in which fantasy was going to be present in the story when he planned it, the mixture between both fictional worlds. We can notice two meaningful elements in that part of the reading: the green velvet armchair and the fact that he has his back toward the door so he cannot be interrupted in his reading. When the killer, who belongs to the secondary fiction, comes totally into the reader's world, he will enter precisely through that door, and will find him with his back toward the door. The bases for fantasy are already set: there is a reader who tries all the possible means to focus and enter the world of the novel, but the extraordinary thing here is that the novel's world ends up entering the reader's world.

He remembered effortlessly the names and his mental image of the characters; the novel spread its glamour over him almost at once. He tasted the almost perverse pleasure of disengaging himself line by line from the things around him, and at the same time feeling his head rest comfortably on the green velvet of the chair with its high back, sensing that the cigarettes rested within reach of his hand, that beyond the great windows the air of the sunset danced under the oak trees in the park. (Cortázar, 1964)

It was not difficult for the novel to seduce the reader; he had already looked for the appropriate place to read the final chapters and remembered the events of the novel. He is surrounded by comfort, and the surrounding objects are directly linked to pleasure. Let's think about the softness of velvet, cigarettes within reach of his hands, and even in the image of the air, which is portrayed as a person dancing; everything helps to create an illusion of pleasure. The use of the metaphor *disengaging himself line by line*, on the one hand, shows us how the reader detaches from his environment, and on the other hand, prepares the field so the narrator begins to tell the story that was happening inside the novel. Another meaningful element on this paragraph in the service of fantasy is the reference to the time of the day in which the events occur. In the primary fiction, events occur in the sunset, while in the secondary fiction, we are told that it is beginning to get dark. If we pay attention to the fictions about to blend, we notice that it is the same hour, and that continuity is also present in this aspect.

> *Word by word, licked up the sordid dilemma of the hero and heroine, letting himself be absorbed to the*

point where the images settled down and took on color and movement, he was witness to the final encounter in the mountain cabin (Cortázar, 1964)

This section is pretty important, for it closes the first moment of the story. We have witnessed the presentation of the reading man and his world and surroundings. We have witnessed how the writer has been preparing the immersion into the secondary fiction, to the events that happen in the novel that is being read. The first line in which the novel is alluded to is "sordid dilemma of the hero and heroine", and there we face the secondary fiction. It is in this part of the story where we find grammatical alternation between both worlds. On the one hand, we have a character that lets himself "be absorbed", and similar expressions referring to the primary fiction; on the other hand, we have the "sordid dilemma of the hero and the heroin", and the "color and movement" of the images that belong to the second fictional world.

The plot of the novel which amazes and absorbs the reader is referring to a very special encounter. The characters in the secondary fiction are facing a "sordid" dilemma, which implies the characters are in the middle of something shady, evil.

Another anticipation of what is about to happen in the continuation of the second part of the story is the fact that the images of the novel "took color and movement", as if they were coming alive, and the reader becomes a mere spectator, that is why Cortázar chooses the word "witness" to allude to the reader in the final paragraph of the moment. In order to be a witness of something, he must be present in the place of the events, and this reader is so immerse in his reading that he feels as if he were watching the happenings. At last, he refers the place where the events of the secondary fiction are taking place.

The woman arrived first, apprehensive; now the lover came in, his face cut by the backlash of a branch. Admirably, she stanched the blood with her kisses, but he rebuffed her caresses, he had not come to perform again the ceremonies of a secret passion, protected by a world of dry leaves and furtive paths through the forest. The dagger warmed itself against his chest, and underneath liberty pounded, hidden close. (Cortázar, 1964)

First thing we notice when we face this second moment of the story's internal structure, is the change in the narrator's point of view. The events being told now are the same events that the character is reading, and we become "witnesses" of this images that have taken color and movement. In this part, we meet the hero and heroine whom have decided to meet in that cabin to solve that "sordid dilemma".

They are a couple of lovers who use this lonely place for their love encounters, but it seems that in this occasion, the purpose of the meeting is quite different. The presentation of these characters is made directly, we get to know them by their actions, and there are no physical or psychological descriptions of any of the characters, just like the reading character.

The woman arrived first to the cabin, but she seemed to be suspicious, prevented, and afraid of the meeting. When her lover arrives, she sees that he is hurt by the lash of a branch; a signal of how dense is the vegetation in the proximities of the cabin. There is an interesting scene where vampirism is present, and it happens when the woman stops her lover's bleeding just by kissing him; in this part, blood can work as a symbolic element that, on the one hand, refers to the passion of the lovers, and on the other hand, is giving us a clue about the death to come. The man rejects her caresses; it shows that this encounter will be different than the others, they will carry out a transcendental action, and it is not just a regular encounter like the others. There is a dagger, as a symbol of freedom, a dagger that is getting warm, and also a prosopopoeia in the concept of freedom, assuming that liberty is hidden, waiting for the moment to give the final blow.

> *A lustful, panting dialogue raced down the pages like a rivulet of snakes, and one felt it had all been decided from eternity. Even to those caresses which writhed about the lover's body, as though wishing to keep him there, to dissuade him from it; they sketched abominably the fame of that other body it was necessary to destroy. Nothing had been forgotten: alibis, unforeseen hazards, possible mistakes.* (Cortázar, 1964)

The use of the prosopopoeia can be seen in this part of the story too, now the writer gives human characteristics to the dialogue of the novel. This dialogue is "lustful", wishful, and it is at the same time compared to a "rivulet of snakes", which implies that it is dangerous and treacherous.

We are told that the dialogue "raced down the pages", and this pages are none but the reader's novel, something that takes us back to the primary fiction amidst this second moment of the story. It is very important that, as readers, we do not miss the fact that the lovers of the cabin are characters of a secondary fiction, and that is why the narrator reminds it referencing the pages of the novel.

The concept of "destiny" is present in the sentence "and one felt it had been decided from eternity", the actions being taken by the characters and the passive attitude of the reader towards the happenings in which he will end up involved, he had no idea that he was ""that other body it was necessary to destroy".. The efforts of the woman to stop her lover were worthless, it was necessary to reach the objective: freedom; it had all been decided from eternity.

> *Nothing had been forgotten: alibis, unforeseen hazards, possible mistakes. From this hour on, each instant had its use minutely assigned. The cold-blooded, twice-gone-over reexamination of the details was barely broken off so that a hand could caress a cheek. It was beginning to get dark.* (Cortázar, 1964)

This is the last part of the narration's second moment in its internal structure. Everything is ready for the final step, the fantastical mixture of both realities. The lovers of the cabin have everything carefully planned: "Alibis, unforeseen hazards, possible mistakes". Amidst this meticulous planning, they only had time to show their passion to each other.

Other meaningful element in the final part of the second moment is the reference to the time of the day in which the facts happen. Let's remember that the reader sat in front of the oak's park at "sunset", and the lovers are ready to act when "It was beginning to get dark", which means the time of the day is the same in both fictions.

> *Not looking at each other now, rigidly fixed upon the task which awaited them, they separated at the cabin door. She was to follow the trail that led north. On the path leading in the opposite direction, he turned for a moment to watch her running, her hair loosened and flying.* (Cortázar, 1964)

This is the beginning of the story's second paragraph, which coincides with the third moment of the internal structure. We have arrived to the point where the fantasy will definitely happen, where impossible things will occur, where two fictions will be mixed and continued.

Now the lovers are only physically apart, because they are "rigidly fixed upon the task" of the assassination. The only moment that might not have a specific task is when the man turns his head to look at his lover and her loose hair. It feels like if the image of his lover encourages him to commit the crime that will lead them to an ultimate freedom.

> *He ran in turn, crouching among the trees and hedges until, in the yellowish fog of dusk, he could distinguish the avenue of trees which led up to the house.* (Cortázar, 1964)

At the beginning of this literary analysis, when I stated the main topic of the story, I said that it was about the continuity established between two fictional worlds; I also added that continuity was conceived precisely in the parks that end up mixing. Well, those trees, hedges and furtive paths among the trees he is reading in his novel, are precisely the surroundings of his home.

The trees surrounding the mountain's cabin, secondary fiction, are continued in the trees that lead to the author's home, primary fiction. "Yellowish fog of dusk" fills the scene with a fantastic nature, generating an indefinite where continuity is possible.

> *The dogs were not supposed to bark, and they did not bark. The estate manager would not be there at this hour, and he was not there. He went up the three porch steps and entered. The woman's words reached him over a thudding of blood in his ears: first a blue chamber, then a hall, then a carpeted stairway. At the top, two doors. No one in the first room, no one in the second. The door of the salon, and then, the knife in his hand, the light from the great windows, the high*

back of an armchair covered in green velvet, the head of the man in the chair reading a novel. (Cortázar, 1964)

This last fragment is very important, as it makes us know the motivation of the crime: love. Even if the woman of the cabin is never linked to the character who reads, she undoubtedly has a sentimental relationship with him. We are not told that this woman is the wife or lover of the reading character, but it is logical to think that he was "*the other body it was necessary to destroy*", so she and her lover can live in absolute freedom. Apart of this, we have enough proof that she knew all of the house's corners perfectly. It's the words of this woman what "reach him over a thudding of blood in his ear", it was her who gave the indications to her lover and partner in crime about how he should proceed and the things he was going to find.

The lover reminds the words of the woman, and the images flow one after another, the killer advances through the house until he reaches the room. The reference to the green velvet armchair is the climax of fantasy, showing that the man who reads the novel is undoubtedly the reading character of the primary fiction. Anyhow, the story has an open ending: everything seems to show that the crime was accomplished, and the man who was sat in the green velvet armchair was reading his own death.

JUAN JOSÉ ARREOLA

The switchman

A disturbing wait between the absurd and fantasy

From a plain satire about the Mexican railway system, going through a critic to dehumanizing mercantilism, the tracks of *The Switchman* (El Guardagujas) end in an allegoric station: mankind's destiny

By: Fernando Chelle

The switchman is a short story by Mexican Juan José Arreola (Ciudad Guzmán, Mexico. September 21st 1918 – Guadalajara, Mexico, December 3rd 2001). This short story is probably the best fantasy short story ever written in Mexico in the 20th century. It was published for the first time in 1952, and is part of a collection named *Confabulario*.

Defining the main topic of this story is not an easy work, for its merit is the multiplicity of interpretations we can give to it; some of them are more evident than the others, but we can say in this story lie many interpretative lines, and all of them are equally valid. Undoubtedly, there is a satire to the Mexican railway system and industrialization; there is also a critic to dehumanizing mercantilism, there is an allegory about mankind's destiny; there is an absurd view on certain political systems and social institutions.

As a resume, we can say that the plot of the story is:

An exhausted stranger carrying his luggage arrives to a deserted train station. It is the exact departure time of his train. Suddenly, he feels that somebody he had not seen before shows himself unexpectedly and taps him. It is a little old man with a vague railway look that has a small red lantern and looks at him anxiously. This two characters immediately start a conversation, as the stranger asks the newly arrived old man if the train to T had already left the station, but the old man, instead of answering him, begins to advice and warn the stranger about different aspects of the weird railway system of that country. In that extensive conversation, the old man, who happens to be a switchman, will tell the stranger an unbelievable, fantastic and absurd story about the railway system. He tells the stranger that the trains in that country do not have a determined schedule and can take the most diverse courses. Sometimes, trains are abandoned and the passengers, once they are helpless, decide to establish new towns. Even in an absurd context, we can see the social inequity, because if there is only one rail and the passengers may get harmed, the first class passengers are on the track where there is still a railway. In this fantastic reality, sometimes, passengers must cooperate with the railway company; passengers even have to do unearthly tasks, like disarming a train piece by piece and take it from one place to another to solve the lack of a bridge. The almighty company recreates a fictitious reality to tranquilize the passengers, using dolls instead of workers and showing paintings of landscapes that pass through the windows and replaces reality. Domestication of the passengers by the company is total; the company has even established schools so the people learn to live together in peace inside the trains. The stranger does not question or doubt about the absurd and fantastic reality the switchman is describing him, but he is somehow chained to his own reality: he wants to get to T; that is the reason why he can only answer that he needs to arrive to T tomorrow. At the end of the story, surprisingly, the train arrives to the station; the old switchman goes away running and jumping all over the railway and tells the stranger that it is his lucky day and he will be in his destiny tomorrow, but when he asks the stranger about his destination again, he does not answer that he needs to get to T, but to the town X. Finally, the switchman disappears, only thing he lefts is the red dot of his lantern floating in the air, while the train was approaching the station noisily.

As I said before, one of the possible interpretations we may get from this story is the satire on the Mexican railway system. The switchman makes a chaotic description showing a brutal disorganization among the employees of the railway company. We can also appreciate a reference to the Mexican industrialization process from the past century. We can also say that this story implies a vast reflection on the implications of industrialization processes in the different societies. The story takes place in a historical time where technological development (related to the means of transport and the industry) had arrived to stay, and mankind saw such advances as a promise of a world full of progress and welfare. However, in Arreola's story, this upcoming technology and machines seem to play a negative and dehumanizing role in the life of the individuals. Men have created machines to take advantage of their services, but this story shows exactly the opposite thing, we see that people live in a world structured for the machines, and it is the people who must adapt to the parameters this new world has imposed. This adaptation and submission that mankind is facing can be clearly seen in the switchman's words, who never criticizes the new social behavior imposed by the railway company; he is even devoted to praise the absurd initiatives the company is carrying on in order to control their passengers. This new historical scenario does not abolish inequalities in that society, as we see there are still privileges and categories in the railway world.

There is also an evident critic to a dehumanizing mercantilism. This can be seen in the description the switchman does on social relationships. Passengers seem to agree with the rules the company has imposed, willingly accepting their own torture.

I also pointed the allegory to the mankind's destiny as one of the possible interpretations. The travel by train might be compared to the travel of the man through life itself, or the different travels a man must make through all the paths of life. If we follow this interpretative path, mankind must accept the conditions life gives them, as well as the stranger must resign his will to get to a specific place and accept the unexpected destinations where the trains might take him. Although the stranger has a ticket destined to T and expects to get to that city, it is not sure at all that his trip will end up arriving that place. The same can happen to every human being, and the teaching of the story seems to the be the importance of getting on the train, living, trying to enjoy the ride, it does not matter if we get to the destination we wanted in the first place, we must be prepared for the possible detours we can face on our way. In this life, human beings tend to suffer the same uncertainty the stranger is facing: loneliness, dismay, bafflement; but life, as well as the train, can have unexpected destinations. According to this interpretation, we can see how every man must take the train, even if they are not sure when will the train come, and not even sure that the train is coming indeed, although they had the precaution of getting a ticket. Maybe we can end up facing the same obstacles than the passengers who established the town F when their train lost its way, others might get to their expected station, but nobody can be sure about it.

A similar view can refer us to the concept of the absurd: even if we can make an interpretation of the train journey as the journey of life, we can interpret it as a journey through the existence of the absurd. It is not logical or rational the fact that the stranger still wants to get on the train, even after hearing the descriptions made by the switchman, and the stranger does not even ask about the amount of mad stories he is hearing, he just wants to get to T. On the other hand, we see that the other passengers accept the terms and conditions of the railway company, they accept to disarm a train that might not take them to their destinations and take it to the other side of a cliff, they accept the fact that they might die there and be buried in cemetery wagons, they definitely accept the establishment of the absurd.

I also find interest in giving a look to the concept of fantasy present on the story, I would like to notice how in this text, that seems realistic in its beginning, ends up little by little, turning into a fantastic story as the switchman talks. There are two different approaches: on one hand, we have an unbelievable story, told by the switchman, who tries to warn the stranger about the characteristics of that country's railway system; on the other hand, we have the story of this stranger who expects to get on a determined train to arrive to an already determined place, the town named T. In this order of ideas, the switchman represents the fantasy, and the stranger represents the normality, the believable things. The switchman has a discourse that relies on the fantasy, and is not opposed only to the reality of the stranger, it is also opposite to the reality we all readers know and recognize as possible. We are all aware that the service provided by the train companies is agreed in advance, functional and unchangeable unless there is a notification of an unexpected change. In normal circumstances, logic says that you buy a ticket for a train that will take you to a previously determined place, that train will use previously placed tracks so everything goes on as intended. Therefore, the stories told by the switchman are totally unbelievable and impossible. Tracks cannot be modified, neither the way the railway system works, for this is an established service and the passengers already know that. However, the stranger's acceptance of the things he is being told gives the reader a perception that the story will transit a different road than the reality he knows, and the reader will finally accept the logic of absurdity that the switchman represents. "The switchman" starts in a recognizable reality, but it stirs to fantasy, it comes back to the recognizable reality when the whistle that announces the arrival of the train is heard. By the way, there is a strange element of the end: when the switchman asks the stranger about his destination, he changes his initial answer: instead of answering T, he ends up saying that he needs to get to X, causing a break in his realistic discourse.

In order to conclude, I will briefly refer the clear influence of Franz Kafka in this story. In the first place, the wait and uncertainty that the stranger suffers can be compared to the difficulties the protagonist of "The castle" experiences. In that novel, we witness the way the protagonist named K is unable to enter a castle where he had the obligation to go. This Kafkaesque character suffers an endless wait that can be compared to the stranger's one. In another kafka's short story named "A common confusion", we can also see the way the dealers A and B arrange a meeting, but they cannot meet each other. The recurrent topic of an endless wait can also be seen in a short story named "Before the law", in which a farmer waits during all of his life an authorization to go through a door. Another typical feature in Kafka's literature that can be seen in the works of Arreola is the tendency towards the infinite and the chaos, a topic that has been approached by the Czech author in "The great wall of China" about that never-ending project, and also in "The city coat of arms", in which he wrote about the impossibility of completing Babel's tower. In Arreola's short story, infiniteness and chaos are present in the railways, as well as the uncountable troubles the passengers must go through. At last, one of the pillar topics in Kafka's literature that can also be seen in "The switchman" is the topic of the indefinable power. This is a recurrent topic in the works of the Czech author that describes the reality of bureaucracy and the big almighty companies, in the short story by Arreola, the national railway company is the one which holds unlimited power.

GABRIEL GARCÍA MÁRQUEZ (I)

A magic story telling

Nobel Prize in literature winner and a master among novelists. Short stories are present through all of Gabo's writing career, from his first works published in Colombian newspapers to *Memoria de mis putas tristes (Memories of my melancholy whores),* his last novel, published in 2004*.* In this article: a sneak peek his short stories, his short stories collection *Los funerales de la Mama Grande (Big Mama's funeral)* and in the article to come: a literary analysis of the short story: *Un día de estos (One of these days).*

By: Fernando Chelle

Gabriel García Márquez and short stories

It is normal and almost logical, that when we think about Gabriel García Márquez (Aracataca, Colombia, March 6th 1927 – México City, México, April 17th 2015), first thing we think about is in a great novelist, awarded Nobel Prize in literature in the year 1982. His ability as a novel writer is beyond question: from *La Hojarasca (Leaf storm, 1955)* to *Memories of my melancholy whores (2004),* passing through the mythic *Cien años de soledad (One hundred years of solitude, 1967)* or any of his other seven novels, the Colombian writer got a well-deserved recognition as a great novelist among literary critics and readers as well. However, short stories are the foundation of his great literature. Short stories are not present exclusively in Gabo's four short stories collection, they can also be found in most of his novels, movie scripts and journalism works. García Márquez himself acknowledged more than once that it is the "little stories" that make the world interesting and fantastic. In his biography *Vivir para contarla (Living to tell the tale, 2002)* as well as in different interviews, García Márquez said that the war stories and anecdotes told to him by his grandfather, whom he called *Papalelo,* and the fantastic stories about ghostly apparitions told by the women who lived in his home came together in his mind and became raw material for his stories, playing a very important role in his literary universe. Even if it is true that García Márquez began his literary adventure the same way many other writers did, writing poetry and later with some humoristic comments, his first relevant literature contributions were his short stories. His first acknowledged short story was called *Psicosis obsesiva (Obsessive Psychosis),* a fantasy story dating back to his high school years in the Liceo Nacional de Varones de Zipaquirá. The most recognized Colombian writer ever started writing short stories in 1947. His first short stories were published by the newspaper *El Espectador* in Bogota, his first short story published was *La tercera resignación (The third resignation)*, and his last one was published in 1955. His first stories were collected and published in a book named *Ojos de perro azul (Eyes of a blue dog)*. A new stage of his writing began when he left Bogota and started working as a journalist in Barranquilla and Cartagena, in the Colombian Caribbean coast. The short story *Un día después del sábado (A day after Saturday)* was awarded the first prize in a short story contest organized by the Asociación de Escritores y Artistas de Colombia (Colombian Writers and Artists' Association) and can be found in the compilation *Tres cuentos colombianos (Three Colombian short stories)* published in 1954. In 1959, when Garcia Marquez was back living in Bogota, he published *Big mama's funeral;* this story is a clear prequel to *One hundred years of solitude*, and is part of a short story collection with the same name. I will further analyze this short story collection because I will make a literary analysis on the short story *Un día de estos (One of these days)*, which is present in said collection. At the end of the 60's, the Colombian Nobel Prize winner began writing a series of short stories that some experts in his works say where destined to be part of a children's book that was never published. These stories were meant to be cinematographic scripts at first, but were finally published in the year of 1972 with the name *La increíble y triste historia de la cándida Eréndira y su abuela desalmada* (*The Incredible and Sad Tale of Innocent Eréndira and Her Heartless Grandmother*). His final short story collection was published in 1992 with the name *12 cuentos peregrinos (Strange pilgrims),* a collection of stories about Latin-American immigrants in Europe, published five hundred years after the European arrival to America.

Big Mama's funeral

Big Mama's funeral is the first short story collection by Colombian writer Gabriel García Márquez, published in 1962. Even if those were not the first short stories written by the Nobel Prize winner, they were the first ones published as a whole book. In this collection we can find seven short stories and a long story (which some critics prefer to call "short novel") titled *Big Mama's funeral,* which is the final story in the book. The scenario for this short story is the small town Macondo, which we had already visited in *Leaf storm* (1955), and we see it again in his most known novel *One hundred years of solitude* (1967). Mario Benedetti said in 1972 that this collection served as a "trampoline for the great imagination spring" of writing that *One hundred years of solitude was.* This sentence by Benedetti is totally true, for in *Big Mama's funeral* we can see certain features that will later appear on *One hundred years of solitude:* the town of Macondo, characters like Colonel Aureliano Buendía and his brother José Arcadio. There are also some stories that García Márquez approached in *La mala hora (In evil hour)*, a novel published in 1962, and in *One hundred years of solitude. Big Mama's funeral* is a book in which we can already see the elements of the magic realism that featured in many of the further García Márquez's works. We find stories that happen in an atmosphere of a heat so intense that surpasses reality. Among the stories we can find in this book there are: a woman who dies 92 years old as a virgin and many important people like the country's president and the pope attend her funeral; a priest who claims to have seen the devil; and a story where many birds fall upon the town (tearing mosquito nets and wired fences apart) among others. All of these stories have an omniscient narrator, who tells the stories in an organized way, which allows an easy reading. As a typical García Márquez work, there are not many dialogues or monologues. Descriptions of the environments where the actions happen are a very relevant element, and are present in all of the stories of this book. Beneath the pages of this short story collection, we can see a parade of many kinds of characters, members of a privileged society as well as the marginal people. We find widows, thieves, carpenters and dentists, as well as politicians, lieutenants, doctors and priests.

One of these days

"A reality not of paper, but one that lives within us and determines each instant of our countless daily deaths, and that nourishes a

source of insatiable creativity, full of sorrow and beauty…"[2]

Gabriel García Márquez, Fragment of the Nobel Prize acceptance's speech

1982

I chose a story named *One of these days* for a literary analysis. This short story is present in the book *Big Mama's funeral* (published by Universidad Veracruzana de Xalapa in 1962).

[2] Translation hosted in
http://www.nobelprize.org/nobel_prizes/literature/laureates/1982/marquez-lecture.html

GABRIEL GARCÍA MÁRQUEZ (II)

A magic story telling

Nobel Prize in literature and a master among novelists. Short stories are present through all his writing career, from his first works published in Colombian newspapers to *Memoria de mis putas tristes (Memories of my melancholy whores),* his last novel, published in 2004. In this article: a literary analysis of the short story *One of these days.*

By: Fernando Chelle

One of these days

"A reality not of paper, but one that lives within us and determines each instant of our countless daily deaths, and that nourishes a source of insatiable creativity, full of sorrow and beauty..."[3]

Gabriel García Márquez, Fragment of the Nobel Prize acceptance's speech

1982

One of these days is part of a short story collection named *Big Mama's funeral* (published by Universidad Veracruzana de Xalapa in Mexico, in 1962).

This short story by Colombian Nobel Prize winner, in which nothing is missing or lacking is strongly linked to the short story *Espuma y*

---

[3] Translation hosted in
http://www.nobelprize.org/nobel_prizes/literature/laureates/1982/marquez-lecture.html

131

nada más (Lather and nothing else), by colombian writer Hernando Téllez. In Téllez's short story, published in his book titled *Cenizas para el viento y otras historias (Ashes for the wind and other stories)* in 1950, we can see a barber and a Captain which can be compared to García Marquez's dentist and military mayor from *One of these days*. Both stories occur somewhere around the 20th century, and allude to the armed conflict in the society, but in Téllez's short story, the role played by the characters is more explicit.

The plot of *One of these days* is the meeting between an empirical dentist and the town's mayor, a military, in an old dental's office where the mayor's tooth will be extracted. There are only three characters, two main characters, Mr. Aurelio Escovar (dentist) and the mayor (lieutenant); and one secondary character, the dentist's son, which works as an intermediary between both parts. Behind this daily life encounter, there is a background full of social violence, corruption, abuse of power, tension and hostility between the main characters.

As well as all the other stories from *Big Mama's funeral,* this short story has a few dialogues and an omniscient third person narrator. It is a linear narration, with only one scenario and action.

The main plot of this story is the concerted truce amidst the ideological conflict between the folk (represented by the dentist) and the government (represented by the mayor) and the inversion of roles, in which the folk, at least for a few moments will impose their rules.

We can see three internal moments. In the first moment, we are introduced to the dentist and his work environment. There is a second moment, the longest one, in which we find the dialogue between the dentist and his son, the irruption of the mayor in the dentist's office and the further removal of his tooth. The third moment of the story is the final short dialogue between the main characters.

The beginning of the story shows a daily life environment, everything seems to be calmed, we can even perceive a nice atmosphere. The omniscient narrator tells us the characteristics of the dentist. The treatment made by the narrator of this character (representation of the folk) is very important, for we receive meaningful details from him, while we barely know about the mayor-lieutenant (representation of the government). The dentist has a name (Aurelio Escovar), the narrator says he is an early bird, working man, organized, methodical and observant. In this part of the story, we do not only know about the dentist, we are also introduced to the scenario where the action will take part. The second moment begins when Escovar's son speaks. The intermediation of the kid, of which we can only hear his voice, shows an unfriendly relationship between the dentist and the lieutenant and the animosity between them. The kid lets his father know that the mayor requires the doctor's professional service: he needs to have a tooth removed. At first, the dentist refuses to take care of the mayor, and tells the kid to let know the mayor that he is not at home, but the mayor listens to the dentist's voice and threatens to shoot at him if he does not pull the foul tooth. Escovar's refusal to take care of his visitor, as well as the expression "So much the better" about the mayor knowing that he is indeed at his office, shows a clear opposition from the dentist against the power of the military. There are elements in the story that allows us suppose things that are not shown explicitly in the reading. Escovar has a gun, this not only shows that he is willing to go against the orders of the mayor, it also shows that he is ready for a military event. Maybe he belongs to a certain resistance group, it is impossible to know, even though after he pulls the mayor's tooth he says "Now you'll pay for our twenty dead men". The mayor has a stereotypical way to belong for a military: he is prepotent, arrogant, and is not afraid to impose his will through violence. But the events of the story do not follow the path we as readers expected. Before defying the mayor to shoot, Escovar made sure that he had his own gun in the lower drawer of his desk. The mayor enters the office after threatening the dentist with shooting him, so the most logical event would have been a shootout between both characters. But nothing of this happens. The doctor sees the marks of pain in the mayor's face and feels sorry for him, and ends up taking care of him normally. But we see the mayor was not happy either with the visit, he spent five painful nights before going to the dentist. Most probably, Escovar was the only dentist in town, but even if he was a self-made dentist, he knew how to do his job.

The conflict in this story is about health, not about politics or a military subject, so the characters must try and interact in the most civilized way they can. This situation leads to a role inversion in the dentist's office, in relation to power. The military is now in the hands of the dentist, and has no option but to obey if he wants his toothache to stop. That is the reason why I said in the beginning of this article that the story was about the folk imposing its rules for a moment. Anyway, the social conflict goes on. Escovar, knowing that this situation was temporary, handles it to his favor. He boils his instruments and retrieves them with cold tweezers without a single sign of hurry, washes his hand while the desperate mayor is staring at him. He even has an excuse to inflict extra pain to the mayor: the tooth has an abscess, so it must be pulled out without using anesthesia. The existence of the abscess is left to our imagination, it is never confirmed. The confirmed fact here is the big amount of pain the mayor will go through. His pain will be so intense that the dentist says him "Now you'll pay for our twenty dead men, lieutenant". It is totally meaningful that the dentist calls the mayor by his military rank. The dentist is charging the mayor with twenty dead men, which might mean that the mayor-lieutenant is responsible for their deaths, and the dentist says "our twenty dead man", in plural, which might mean that these dead people are part of the folk. After the dentist pulls the foul tooth out, he offers the mayor a dry and clean handkerchief. The dentist specifies the mayor that the piece of cloth is for drying his tears, in contrast to the typical arrogant attitude of the military.

The last moment of the story comes in the form of a small dialogue between the characters. In this segment, political corruption in that violent society is made evident. That military, who probably seized power with the help of guns and submits the town with the power of violence, who has killed at least tens of people, finances his personal account with the municipal treasury. He feels no shame in admitting that he and the city hall are "the same damn thing".

CLARICE LISPECTOR (I)

The non-style of the internal world

Clarice Lispector was a Brazilian writer born in Ukraine, in a Jewish family. She is one of the most important short story writers in the 20th century in her country and in Portuguese language. This two-part article will approach her biography, works, short stories, and will make a further analysis on one of her most representative short stories: *Clandestine happiness.*

By: Fernando Chelle

Since September 2014, when I started my collaboration with **Vadenuevo**, I focused my attention on different Latin-American short story writers. Although this has not been the only topic I have worked on, as I have written about Kafka's *The Metamorphosis*, about the Parlamento Nacional de Escritores de Colombia (Colombia's National Writers Congress), and other kinds of literary manifestations such as utopias, dystopias and uchronies, the truth is that Latin-American short story writers have the biggest percentage of attention in my works. My articles about Felisberto Hernández, Julio Cortázar and Jorge Luis Borges are now part of a book published on May 2015, named **The fantastic short story in Rio de la Plata.** After publishing this work about authors from the region of Rio de la Plata, I thought about a more ambitious idea: to study different Latin-American short stories for the magazine and then add them to a compilation named "*The Latin American Short Story*" or something like it. I have noticed that there are many books about fantastic short stories in Rio de la Plata as well as Latin American short stories, but my works are not author's compilations with dates and characteristics, my works are an analytic and personal look of those texts. Thinking about this new ambitious idea, I decided to start analyzing some short stories by Latin American writers that did not belong to the region of Rio de la Plata. After leaving my nearest geography, my first stop was Mexico. For my literary project, all of the countries bring a difficulty: each one of them has many good writers, and I can only choose one. Once the author is chosen, I find a second difficulty: I have to choose the short story. This is not an easy task. In this case, I try to choose one of the most representative short stories of each country. In Mexico, I chose Juan José Arreola and his short story *The Switchman*. I continued my search through Latin America and I stopped in Colombia, the country in which I have lived for the past five years. Even though Colombia has a great amount of good short story writers, it was not very difficult to choose the most representative one. I decided to study a short story by Gabriel García Márquez named *One of these days.* I will keep doing the same with every Latin American country until I finish the book I planned. Of course I will keep publishing alternately analysis on short stories as well as other topics I consider relevant in certain issues. For example, my article about Julio Cortázar coincides with his 100th birthday; the chronic about *The Metamorphosis* coincides with the 100th year since its publication, the chronic about the Parlamento Nacional de Escritores de Colombia was published one month after the event, and in the months to come I am planning to publish an article about the 50th anniversary since the publication of Truman Capote's *In cold blood,* and so on. Once I have explained this, it is time to focus on the country, the author and the short story I have chosen for this month's article.

Continuing my literary journey through the Latin American short story, it's time for Brazil. To choose on Brazilian representative short story is not as easy as it was for Colombia. There are many authors that I could have chosen: Joaquim Machado de Assis, João Guimarães Rosa, Carlos Drummond de Andrade or Jorge Amado himself, just for naming a few of the representative writers in this large country. I ended up choosing a short story by the great Ukrainian born Clarice Lispector (Chechelnik, Ukraine, December 10th 1920 – Rio De Janeiro, Brasil, December 9th 1977). I chose, for the literary analysis, a short story named *Clandestine happiness,* the first short story of a collection with the same name, published in Rio de Janeiro in 1971.

The author

Clarice Lispector, born Chaiuya Pinkhasovna Lispector on December 1920 in Chechelnik, Ukraine, she was a Jewish descendant writer. She landed in Brazil, more specifically in the city of Recife when she was a few months old. Her mom died when she was just ten years old. Her writing vein was seen very early in her life. She began mailing stories to the Pernambuco's Newspaper, but they were rejected for being considered a mere feeling's expression without narrative action. This early characteristic was still present during her whole literary career and is one of the main features in her narrations. When she was fourteen, she moved with her family to Rio De Janeiro, where she studied Law and began to collaborate with some magazines and newspapers. In 1943 she published a novel named *Near to the wild heart,* which granted her first literary award, the Fundación Graça Aranha Prize for best book of the year. In the same year she married a College classmate, the diplomat Maury Gurgel Valente with whom she lived in different countries (Italy, England, France and finally Switzerland, where their first son Paulo was born). In 1946 she published her second novel *O lustre (The chandelier)*. Clarice exchanged letters almost daily with the writer Fernando Sabino, she felt unhappy in foreign lands and homesick for Brasil. She returned to Rio de Janeiro in 1949 where she returned to journalistic labor, using the penname Tereza Quadros. The destiny obliged her to live outside Brazil once more, she moved with her husband to the USA in 1952, and one year later her second son, Pedro, was born. She lived in the USA for seven years and became friend with Brazilian writer Érico Veríssimo. She never stopped publishing in Brazilian media, neither exchanging letters with other writers like Otto Lara Resende. Her literary recognition arrived in 1954 when *Near the wild heart* was translated into the French language, with a cover painted by Henri Matisse.

Clarice Lispector divorced in 1959 and went back to Rio de Janeiro where she started a productive and successful stage. In 1960 she published the successful *Family Ties,* her second short story collection. Then in 1961 she published her novel *The apple in the dark* and in 1963, the novel considered her masterpiece *The passion according to G.H.*

In September 1966, Lispector was rescued from a fire in her room; she fell asleep with a lit cigarette in her hand which caused the fire. She spent some months in a hospital recovering from the burns, but she still had traces that accompanied her until her death. Her body, as well as her works, was marked by this tragic event. She died in Rio de Janeiro, in December 1977, victim of an ovaries cancer; she was 56 years old. She died a few months after the publication of her last novel: *The hour of the star.*

Her short stories

The first short story collection published by Clarice Lispector is a compilation of six stories that features some characteristics for which she was rejected by the Newspaper of

Pernambuco. These are short stories where the action seems to be left aside and privileges the characters' feelings and sensations. The collection was published in 1952 and is titled: *Some stories.*

As I said earlier in this article, in 1960, *Family ties*, her second short story collection, was published with a lot of success. *Family ties* is about her family life and her complex personality. Brazilian writer Érico Verissimo, her great friend in USA, said once that this book was "the best short story collection since Machado de Assis". Her next short story collection was published in 1964 and was titled *The foreign legion,* it has 13 short stories. Her following short story compilation was named *Clandestine Happiness,* it was published in 1971. It is a very intimate book, and one of Clarice's best known work; the homonymous short story is the first one in that book, and is the one I chose for a further analysis in the second part of this article.

In 1974 Clarice Lispector published one of her two most controversial short story collections: *The Via Crucis of the body, Where you were at night*, where we can find erotic and sexual short stories. Her short stories collection ended when she published the book *Beauty and the beast*, a compilation published by her son that gathers texts from her initial and final years.

Narrative features

Clarice Lispector said once that her writing style was a non-style. She was always more interested in the psychological development of her characters than in the narrative actions of the story. Therefore, she was compared by some critics with other writers such as Virginia Woolf or James Joyce. Her short stories are always showing the inside mind of the characters, their mental processes and personal experiences. The thoughts of the characters on certain situations are always more important than the situations themselves. The intimate life of the characters is the most important feature in her stories, their fears, secrets and else; the events only matter as long as the characters' thoughts on them are relevant. In her short stories we can find different tones, some of them are erotic, others can be sad or funny, but always take action in daily-life environments, where the characters' impressions and sensations are shown. Her stories often take place in domestic spaces, where daily-life events happen, and it is there when her characters (mostly female) project their inner selves and show their emotions. Her interest in describing the sensations and desires of the intimate life is clearly seen in *Clandestine happiness,* the short story I chose for an analysis. It is a short story that takes a look into a child's mind, the thoughts and feelings of a girl. It is a story about cruelty and pain, but also about joy and passion.

Clandestine Happiness

CLARICE LISPECTOR (II)

The non-style of the internal world

With excerpts of the translation from the Portuguese by Rachel Klein in http://bombmagazine.org/article/7108/clandestine-happiness

Clarice Lispector was a Brazilian writer born in Ukraine, in a Jewish family. She is one of the most important short story writers in the 20th century in her country and in Portuguese language. This is the second part of a work that studies her biography, works, stories and style, a literary analysis of one of her most representative short stories: *Clandestine happiness.*

By: Fernando Chelle

"A woman's look and maybe a woman's writing style too. Clarice Lispector impregnated the world with her smart woman's view, able to perceive the most minimal sensations and knowing that nothing is irrelevant, no matter how small or trivial it is. The daily-life world, the world of those things that have no story, it has been the woman's world for a long time, but it can provide us with innumerable surprises, it only takes a deep look and understanding of the signs of an underlying reality"

Elena Losada Soler

The purpose of this article is to continue the previous one on **Vadenuevo,** about Brazilian Ukrainian born writer Clarice Lispector

(Chechelnik, Ukraine, December 10th 1920 – Rio de Janeiro, Brazil, December 9th 1977). I will make a literary analysis on her short story *Clandestine Happiness,* the initial short story of a homonymous book published in Rio de Janeiro in 1971.

The main plot of the story is about evil, moral suffering and humiliation inflicted to a little girl by her classmate. The antagonist of the story is a fat, short, freckled and big breasted girl who, driven by jealousy of the other schoolgirls, begins a sort of sadistic and evil vengeance on a girl; this plot runs around the possession of a book that the protagonist really wants. The protagonist affords the humiliation, but thanks to her perseverance and the mediation of the evil girl's mother, ends up succeeding and taking possession of the wished book.

The short story has a "Classic structure": beginning, middle and end. In the first moment, the narration introduces the two main characters of the story: in the first place, the antagonist girl and then the protagonist girl, who is also the narrator. This first moment also shows the second moment's point of interest: book loans and sadism towards the protagonist, who wants to read a particular book. The second moment, the longest one in the narration, focuses on what she calls the "Chinese torture", referring to the protagonist persistence in having the book borrowed, a book named *Adventures of Little Nose* by Monteiro Lobato. The plot is solved when the mom of the girl who owns the book shows up in the scene. The final moment of the story focuses in the experiences of the protagonist after she could finally get the book.

A look into the plot and some commentaries.

There are a lot of autobiographic elements in this story. Even if the fiction is as free as the writers want, there is no doubt that the blonde, skinny and tall girl is Clarice Lispector herself when she lived in Recife This short story shows childhood as a stage of exploration and discovery, a preparation for life. On the one hand, it is about the protagonist's hope of getting the book, and on the other hand, the jealous antagonist girl, who humiliates and torments her class mate just for considering her more beautiful. The jealousy and evil of this antagonist drives her to begin some sort of vengeance towards the protagonist, who is a representative of those stylized pretty girls so different to the antagonist herself.

"She was fat, short, freckled and with sort of reddish excessively frizzy hair. She had an enormous bust, while all of us were still flat chested (...) But what a talent she had for cruelty. She was pure vengeance, noisily chewing her caramels. How this girl must have hated us, we who were unforgivably pretty, thin, tall, with smooth hair."

The antagonist, daughter of the bookstore owner, has the advantage of having a book that the protagonist wants, *Adventure of Little Nose* by Monteiro Lobato, a classic Brazilian's child book. The antagonist promises the narrator that she will lend her the aforementioned book, but she uses this power to mercilessly humiliate and inflict moral pain in the narrator. The antagonist starts telling the narrator that she must head to the antagonist's home to get the book borrowed, but days pass and the antagonist always has an excuse for not lending the book, and the same thing happens every day. The evil of the bookstore owner's daughter can be seen in the pleasure she feels by humiliating and tormenting the other girl.

"The secret plan of the bookstore owner's daughter was quiet and diabolic (...) And so it continued. For how long? I went to her house every day, without missing a single day".

We can see how the protagonist, even though she is aware of the torture she is being inflicted, keeps going to the antagonist's house with joy, with the hope of finally receiving the book. The love for reading makes her afford the humiliation, but in the end, the circumstances turn in favor and she ends up being benefited. One day, the mother of the antagonist girl, who has repeatedly seen the other girl in her house's door, and after she asks for explanations, becomes aware of the evil game that her own daughter was playing. As a punishment, the mother gives the book to the protagonist, and tells her that she can keep it all the time she wants.

"for as long as I would like" is all that a *person, big or small, can dare to want."*

This is something wonderful for the blackmail victim; it means that there are no restrictions and boundaries of any kind. Nevertheless, despite we thought the girl was going to start reading immediately, she decided to postpone the reading and just enjoy the possession of the book as a mere object. She prefers to enjoy the emotion of a slow reading, because she will have the book "For as long as she likes". The story ends before the protagonist reads the book entirely, reading becomes to her a clandestine happiness. On the other hand, this short story which shows childhood as a stage of exploration and discovery of life, it ends with a paragraph that sort of shows the end of the childhood, the protagonist's transit to sexual maturity.

"From time to time I sat in the hammock, swaying with the book open on my lap, without touching it, in the purest state of

ecstasy. I was no longer a girl with a book: *I was a woman with her lover."*

AUGUSTO ROA BASTOS

The excavation

A ceaseless fight for freedom and life

War, casualties, tunnels, victims and murderers, plots and a frustrated freedom. *The excavation* is one of the most representative stories by the Paraguayan Cervantes Prize winner.

By: Fernando Chelle

The story chosen for a literary analysis was written by Paraguayan writer Augusto Roa

Bastos (Asunción, Paraguay, June 13th 1917 – idem, April 26th 2005). It is a short story called *La excavación (The excavation)*, a story that belongs to the book *El trueno entre las hojas (Thunder among the leaves),* published by Editorial Losada in 1953.

Thunder among the leaves is one of the most important books by Augusto Roa Bastos, for it was the first book that granted him international recognition. *The excavation* is the fifth story among other seventeen stories in this short story collection. These stories are about politics, cultural, racial and linguistic clash in Paraguay, and the struggle for survival. *Thunder among leaves* is a book fed by the Paraguayan oral-folkloric literature. This book is full of suffering characters which dignity has been taken away. They are men who were violated, who live in the midst of misery and oppression. In this work, Roa Bastos frequently relies in the grotesque element as a descriptive resource, highlighting misery and injustice. In most stories, (*The excavation is an exception*), a natural community is disturbed by the arrival of civilization; in this situation, the primitive community has no choice but to fight against violence, degradation and slavery that comes with the triumph of civilization. The different struggles that are seen throughout the work will be marked by the unfortunate characters' unending optimism.

In *The excavation*, a prisoner named Perucho Rodi, who lives with almost one hundred other prisoners in a cell, finds out that he is living miserably, like a living dead. The story, which refers to Paraguayan internal wars as well as the Chaco War, shows how precarious the Paraguayan jails are, and his main plot is Perucho Rodi's agonic struggle for freedom and a true life. The narrator's omniscient voice sets the structure of the story. The narration begins in present tense, but then there are two retrospective stories: one about the life of the prisoners in the Cell 4, and another about a military operation carried out by the protagonist in the Chaco War.

A sneak peek to the plot

A former Chaco War soldier, whose name is Perucho Rodi, is locked in the overcrowded cell 4 (Valley- i), a place which, in a normal situation, would only host eight prisoners. All of these are political prisoners that have been there for six months after the end of a civil war. In the beginning, there were eighty-nine prisoners, but seventeen have already died, nine of them because of several diseases, four died because of the inflicted tortures, two because of Phthisis and other two committed suicide. The inhuman situation the prisoners suffer and their longing for freedom leads them to organize a jailbreak, excavating a tunnel that allows them to escape the prison. The prisoners take their turns every four hours every day, six men advance fifty centimeters to freedom. Perucho Rodi, the protagonist prisoner, was an engineering student, and also had the experience of having excavated a tunnel during the Chaco War. Now, using only an edge-sharpened dish, excavates a tunnel that, according to his calculations, would lead them from the Cell 4 (Valley-i) to the ravine of the Paraguay River.

The confinement, diseases, tortures and suicides told in this story are absolutely tragic and horrifying. Cell 4 (Valley-i) is a place where men barely survive, sustained only by their hope that someday they will be free again. In the story, there have passed four months of asphyxia and hard work, and there are only five meters left to finish the tunnel, about twenty-five days of work. Roa's story begins with an earth detachment for which he does not care at the beginning. But immediately after, there is a second earth detachment that buries the lower limbs of the digger. As readers, with the description given of the situation, we notice that Rodi is definitely stuck and he will be unable to do anything about it. There is no way he neither comes back to the cell nor gets to the ravine, because the distance is still too long. The narrator, using a free indirect style, begins to show Rodi's thoughts, who still cannot understand clearly what just happened to him. His deep desire for getting to freedom leads him to confusion as well as to excessive hope. As the asphyxiation progresses, the digger begins to remember his time as a soldier in the Chaco War. There is a flashback inside Rodi's mind; it looks as if the tunnel he is digging can only lead him to his memories, where he casually finds another tunnel. In the Chaco War which confronted Paraguayans against Bolivians, in the battlefront of Gondra, the enemy trenches where just fifty meters away. Perucho Rodi, along with fourteen men, dug an eighty meters tunnel during eighteen days, from the Paraguayan trench to the posterior part of the Bolivian rearguard. Thanks to this, Perucho Rodi won the battle, and thanks to this stratagem, the Paraguayan army took their enemy by surprise. Rodi's memories then become a hallucination, a delirium, and the story tends to circularity. Perucho Rodi interprets that the eighty-nine murdered people in the night of Gondra are the same eighty-nine prisoners in the Cell 4 (Valley-i). The faces of the people in the Chaco War are now the faces of his cellmates, and that Bolivian soldier whom he shots to death looks so much like himself that he could have been his own twin.

Perucho Rodi dies by asphyxia. The tunnel does not get him to freedom, neither to his cellmates. It will even become an excuse and cover up for the prison guards to kill the remaining prisoners. When the guards find out the tunnel of the Cell 4 (Valley-i) get a macabre idea. The night after they discover the tunnel, the prisoners see that the door of their cell is unlocked. Despite the unexplainable situation, they do not suspect a possible ambush. They go out, find everything desert, they cross a back door that leads to an alley and they fall right into the trap. They are eliminated in a few seconds by machine gun fire. It is a similar death to that suffered by the Bolivians of the front of Gondra at the hands of Rodi and other Paraguayan soldiers.

The prison guards were able to distort the truth for the public; they had a satisfying explanation of the facts and were able to use the truth in order to lie. There was the tunnel that nobody wanted to look and made the guard's version of a jailbreak believable. The short story's end shows the invariability of the situation in jails, as the tunnel was blocked and later the Cell 4 «got overcrowded again», which shows the beginning of another horrifying cycle.

A small reflection

This is a short story that we can call "a typical Roa Bastos". There is an implicit social protest, the complaint for the living conditions of the underprivileged, the defense of human rights and the fight against injustice. We can also see something I said in the beginning of this article: the hope of the unfortunate character amidst a totally adverse situation. The hope can be seen in the prisoners' decision to dig a tunnel, but it can also be seen in the agonizing Rodi's thoughts. These are thoughts that are not exempts of guilt because, prior to his death, Rodi remembers the killings and deaths in the Chaco war, which torments him. Roa's genius touch can be seen in that game he establishes between the past and the present in Perucho Rodi's mind. This prisoner, who is the protagonist the story, lives a deplorable situation and is also a victim of abuses and injustice is a former killer of eighty-nine Bolivians, whom he murdered in their sleep. Seen that way, he is also a traitor to the human fraternity and it makes him feel guilty. That is why the eighty-nine faces of the Bolivians become the faces of the eighty-nine prisoners in the present, including Perucho Rodi himself, who also sees his own face in the enemy he shot with his machine gun in that unforgettable night at Gondra's battlefront.

ROBERTO BOLAÑO

SENSINI

Excerpts of the translation by: Chris Andrews hosted in
http://www.barcelonareview.com/63/e_rb.html

When literature becomes the search for a decent life instead of glory.

Through his favorite alter-ego, Roberto Bolaño shows the life of two Latin American writers exiled in Spain, by the times of the dictatorships in America's south cone. Under these circumstances, the literary creation, instead of being the search for glory and recognition, becomes the search for the economic prizes that will allow the protagonists to pay the bills. Literary contests, social relationships, exile, you can find all of these in this short story by the writer of *The savage detectives*.

By: Fernando Chelle

Continuing my journey through the vast, rich and diverse world of the Latin American short story, I made a stop in Chile. I will analize a story titled *Sensini*, by Chilean writer Roberto Bolaño (Santiago de Chile, Chile, April 28th 1953 - Barcelona, Spain, July 15th 2003), from the book *Phone calls*, published in Barcelona in 1997 by Editorial Anagrama.

Phone calls was the winner of the Premio Municipal de Santiago de Chile (Municipal Prize of Santiago de Chile), it was the first of four short stories collection by Roberto Bolaño; it was followed by: *Murdering whores* (2001) and two books published posthumously, *The insufferable Gaucho* (2003) and *The secret of evil* (2007). Bolaño's short stories were also collected in a book called *Cuentos*, published in 2013 by Editorial Anagrama in Barcelona, Spain. But let's take a look the book *Phone Calls*, and then we can focus into the comments of *Sensini*. This first book by Bolaño, dedicated to his wife Carolina

Lopez, consists of fourteen stories and is divided into three parts. The writer decided to title each of the parts of the book, just like the title of the story that closes it; for example, the first part is called *Phone calls* just like the fifth story. It is preceded by the tales *Sensini*, *Henri Simon Leprince*, *Enrique Martín* and *Una Aventura literaria (A literary adventure)*. This first part is the one that interested me, not only because it is where *Sensini* and the metaliterary Bolaño can be seen, also because four of the five stories on it have writers as protagonists and their main theme is the literary work. I will leave *Sensini* aside for a moment, for I will give a further look in detail to it later this article. In *Henri Simon Leprince*, the protagonist is a frustrated writer, with few friends and not much capacity of making his works known; *Enrique Martin*, is another unhappy protagonist, a poet who ends up hanging himself in his own bookstore; *A literary adventure* shows a critical confrontation of two antagonistic writers who exchange appreciations; *Phone calls*, the homonymous story to this first part and also the book, is a simple story of dismay that includes the death of one of the parts, it is not a story that addresses the literary subject. The second part of the book, titled *Detectives*, does not address the literary topic; the most frequent topics in the second part are detectives and investigations; and the third part, titled *Anne Moore*, which focuses on stories whose protagonists are women.

In *Sensini*, the first story of *Phone calls*, we know, through the indefatigable Arturo Belano (the favorite Roberto Bolaño's alter-ego), that he needs to take part on literary contests in different parts of Spain in order to complete the necessary money for living, because the scarce savings he got from working as a night watchman in a camping are running out. This story, winner of the San Narrative Prize Ciudad de San Sebastian, takes place at the time when Roberto Bolaño lived in Girona and

Barcelona, where he became acquainted with other exiled Latin American writers.

The theme of the story is the relation between literary creation and the market, while it revolves around literary contests. It unveils the reality of two non-consecrated writers in exile. The main characters do not seek the glory or recognition in the literary contests, but rather some money that allows them to meet the needs of the daily life. In the epistolary exchange between these writers, the triviality of these provincial contests is revealed. In these contests, the jurors do not read the whole works and sometimes they do not even read them. This provokes that the creators take advantage of the irregular situation and do not care about sending the same story with different titles to more than one contest. In this social and literary context, the stories have a pragmatic purpose and, as if they were racehorses, the writers send them to compete for the different cities of the Spanish territory, hoping to win as many awards as possible. It is a story with a strong autobiographical component that allows us to imagine the gestation of some of Bolaño's works, and on the other hand also shows us the difficulties that the writer had to face at certain moments of his life. The protagonists are easily identifiable: on the one hand, Roberto Bolaño (Arturo Belano), who takes the place of narrator protagonist, a young Chilean exiled in Spain; and on the other hand Antonio Di Benedetto (Sensini), a writer who, as well as in the fiction, was exiled in Spain. The epistolary relationship between Antonio Di Benedetto and Roberto Bolaño was really historical, it was real, and it is precisely from that relationship where the Chilean writer took his narrative material from. Although the story is part of *Telephone calls* and was published in 1997, the story told there dates back to the late seventies or early eighties. Considering this autobiographical element, we can see *Sensini* as a sort of fictional game where different layers overlap each other. There is a Bolaño author who signs the work, and who invents Belano, the narrator, inspired in turn by a Bolaño author. The author invents a narrator who tells how he wrote what is published in the end, and that is ultimately what the readers read, some kind of Chinese boxes. Having made this fundamental appreciation, I will analize some aspects of the story's argument.

Sensini is a story narrated in first person by a protagonist narrator. It has a classic structure where the events follow a chronological order.

A young twenty-five-year-old Chilean writer based in Spain discovers that Luis Antonio Sensini, an Argentinian writer whom he admired, had participated in a literary contest where the narrator had obtained a mention, with the difference that the story written by Sensini was superior even to the winning story.

Arturo Belano, the protagonist young man, decides to ask the contest's organizers for Sensini's address. Once he gets it, he writes a letter to him expressing his admiration and comments on some aspects of the said contest. Two weeks later, Belano receives a letter written by Sensini and which begins an epistolary relationship. In their first letters, they just exchange some basic information, mainly about literary contests. The Argentinian writer encourages the narrator to participate in every contest he can. As time goes by, they become closer to each other and Sensini starts telling Belano about different aspects of his life, for example, that he was living with his wife and one daughter, and that he had a son from a previous marriage that was allegedly lost in South America. Sensini also tells Belano about his precarious economic situation. Meanwhile, Belano tries to get deeper into the world of Sensini and begins to read and reread everything he can from the Argentinian author. At one point, on the initiative of Belano, interested in meeting Sensini's daughter, the writers exchange photographs. In a letter, Sensini tells the narrator the corpse of his son was apparently found in a common grave of a clandestine cemetery. Later, when Belano returns to Girona after some time out, he finds a letter from Sensini, where he informs the narrator that he decided to return to Argentina. The dictatorship had fallen and there, he would be able find more clues about his son Gregorio. He returned with his wife, while his daughter remained in Spain. Belano decides to contact the daughter of his epistolary friend, but he does not succeed. Two years later, he gets the news that Sensini is dead, and Belano believes it was logical to think that the writer had decided to go and die in his own country. A short time later, someone knocks on Belano's door: it was Miranda Sensini with a man. Belano prepares dinner and a room for the visitors who were traveling around Europe. Once the visitors go to sleep, Belano, who can't fall sleep, decides to watch TV and remembers Sensini. He then notices that Miranda Sensini could not fall sleep neither, so she comes downstairs and begins to talk with Belano. They talk about Sensini, about his last moments alive, about how much some consecrated authors admired him and the little recognition he had, about the amount of literary contests he had won and about how happy he was with the epistolary relationship he had with Belano.

Two writers in exile

To finish the article, I will quote some passages from the story that refer to the exile .the characters. The story itself has an autobiographical value; it is an extensive testimony of the epistolary exchange between two authors exiled from their own countries. Arturo Belano begins the story making clear his condition of exile.

"I had practically no friends and all I did was writing and go for long walks. I started at seven in the evening, just after getting up, with a feeling like jet lag: an odd sensation of fragility, of being and not being there, somehow distant from my surroundings".

The narrator tells his story from a condition of alienation to the place. But also in the story we can see, at least in their memory, the homelands that they had to abandon because of violence. In the first letter Belano sent to Sensini, it already refers to the political aspect:

"(…) the political situation in Chile and in Argentina (both dictatorships were still firmly in place), life in Spain, and life in general".

Starting from this first letter, we will witness not only a letter exchange by two writers: we will also witness a letter exchange between two exiled Latin Americans in Spain. Sensini's homeland is present in his short stories.

"Although the themes and situations varied, the settings were usually rural, and the protagonists were the fabled horsemen of the pampas, that is to say armed and generally unfortunate individuals, either loners or men endowed with a peculiar notion of sociability."

Friendship arose between these characters because there is an almost total identification to each other. The living conditions they faced were very similar, hence empathy. The letters help these characters to stimulate each other, reflect on their lives and the literary world they also have to share.

One notable aspect of Sensini's life is that he is deeply saddened by the disappearance of his son, a young thirty-five years old journalist. Belano wrote a poem referring to the case of Gregorio and Latin American political reality:

"In the meantime I remember I wrote a very long, very bad poem, full of voices and faces that seemed different at first, but all belonging

to Miranda Sensini, and when, in the poem, I finally realized this and could put it into words, when I could say to her, Miranda it's me, your father's friend and correspondent, she turned around and ran off in search of her brother, Gregorio Samsa, in search of Gregorio Samsa's eyes, shining at the end of a dim corridor in which the shadowy masses of Latin America's terror were shifting imperceptibly."

After some time of uninterrupted letter exchange, when Belano knew about Sensini's death in Argentina, he expressed:

"I don't know why, but it seemed logical that Sensini would go back to Buenos Aires to die."

This is a reflection by someone who is also exiled; that is why Sensini's election of dying in his homeland makes sense to the narrator. For a political exile, returning to his country means to return to what belongs to him but was taken away.

The reflection on Belano's solitude in the foreign country that can be seen from the beginning of the story can be seen again in the end, when Miranda Sensini visits him at his home. When the girl knocks on the door, Belano thinks:

"I knew only a few people in Girona and none of them would have turned up like that unless something out of the ordinary had happened"

It is one of so many sentences that show the reality of exile. It is not easy to fit in a society when you are a foreigner, or when you do not have the contacts that the other inhabitants might have. That is why Belano worked in whatever he could and tried to win literary awards, he tried to survive knowing his condition of foreigner, a condition he shared with the other writer in which he could feel reflected, Luis Antonio Sensini.

MARIO VARGAS LLOSA

On Sunday

A teenage world

In the struggle of a young man for love, Mario Vargas Llosa shows the world of adolescence and the early youth. In this story, we can find the groups of friends and their codes, anguish, fears and rebellion. This story shows how psychological processes occur in this trascendental stage of life.

By: Fernando Chelle

Following the Latin American roads, I got to Peru. Some months ago, when I wrote about Clarice Lispector, I noted how difficult is to choose a specific writer in some countries full of remarkable short story tellers. Peru is one of those cases, and maybe Mario Vargas Llosa (Arequipa, Perú, March 28th 1936) is not as recognized as short storyteller as he is as a novelist, but the Peruvian Nobel Prize winner began his literary work precisely as a short story teller. The short story I chose for the analysis is titled *On Sunday,* which is included in the book *Los Jefes (*translated *The cubs and other short stories)*, originally published in Barcelona in 1959 by Editorial Roca.

The cubs is the first book ever published by Mario Vargas Llosa, it is his only short story collection, and it is a compilation of six short stories: *Los jefes (The cubs), El desafío (The Challenge), El hermano menor (The youngest brother), Día Domingo (On Sunday), Un visitante (A visitor)* and *El abuelo (The Grandfather)*. *The cubs* was as relevant for Vargas Llosa as *Big mama's funeral* for Gabriel García Márquez, for they were trampolines for the imaginative leap of their authors. *The cubs* is a realistic book which shows urban topics characters and landscapes, typical in Vargas Llosa's literary work. This short story collection was awarded the Leopoldo Alas Prize in 1958, and published by Editorial Roca in 1959. There were five short stories in the book originally, all of the aforementioned short stories except for *A visitor;* this short story is included in a Peruvian second edition of 1964 (Populibros Peruanos), and it does not include *The Grandfather*. Its third edition, released in 1965 (José Godard Editor), featured the six definitive stories that have appeared in the further editions. The stories featured in this book are inspired in young Vargas Llosa's own life. These short stories occur in different Peruvian places and were conceived by their author when he was between 17 and 19 years old. The main characters are often young males who meet in groups, a recurrent characteristic in Vargas Llosa's literature. It can be seen in *On Sunday, The cubs* and *The challenge* as well as in his novels *La ciudad y los perros*[4] *(The time of the hero)* and *La casa verde (The green house)*. The events in the stories inside the book is always about a group of young men constantly challenging themselves, in a context of male dominance in which there is a cult for courage and despise for cowardice.

On Sunday is a short story that reflects on the world of a group of teenagers from Lima in the 50's, but its main topics are friendship and the first love. This story can be considered somehow a 'documentary', for it happens in a recognizable place (for Peruvians, mainly),

---

[4] Literally "The city and the dogs"

and it illustrates a determined time and some of its habits.

Plot

The main topic of this story is the rivalry between two young men, Miguel and Ruben, because of their love to a girl named Flora. It begins when Miguel finally gathers some courage and declares his love to Flora. Miguel knew through 'Melanés', one of the members of the group named Los Pajarracos (*The birds*,), that Ruben had the intention to declare his own love to Flora, with his sister Martha as an accomplice. For that reason, and knowing that Ruben was the most popular guy of the school, acknowledging him as a natural born Casanova endowed with a great physical condition that allowed him to become a swimming champion, Miguel decided to rush and declare his love to Flora to be the first one in her consideration. Although the young lady does not reject him, she decides to tell him about her decision in a different moment. When Miguel asks her out to the movies the next Saturday, Flora says that she would be visiting Martha, so Miguel begins to plan a strategy to ruin Ruben and Flora's encounter. First thing he does is to look for Ruben in the bar where The Birds usually meet. In order to stop Ruben from going to Martha's house, Miguel challenges him to see which one of them can drink more beers before passing out. Ruben, who had said at first that he could not stay in the bar, ends up accepting the challenge. Even though there is not a winner in this first challenge, Miguel achieves his purpose of delaying Ruben. But the drinking challenge was not the last one that night: after a series of circumstantial frictions, Ruben challenges Miguel to a swimming competition on the sea, a very dangerous challenge, considering that they were drunk and it was a winter night. Anyway, both challengers accept the "duel" in which the loser had to leave the way clear to the winner, who would be able to make his move on Flora without any obstacle.

Miguel knew well that Ruben was a great swimmer, but the pressure laid on him by his friends made him accept the challenge, because refusing would be unacceptably coward. But his decision to accept the challenge has everything to do with Ruben's promise of leaving Flora alone if he lost. The competitors then headed to the beach and got in the very cold sea, while their friends waited on the strand. After a moment in which nothing relevant seemed to occur, the swimmers began to feel the severity of the frozen water and their organisms got affected by the alcohol and the relentless cold. Miguel then felt cramps and began to lose his ability to move his limbs; he got afraid in a certain moment, for he was not able to see neither his rival nor the strand. Suddenly, he heard the desperate voice of Ruben asking for help, and everything changed, he did not worry for his pain anymore and felt inspired to save his rival-friend. He went floating to the place where Ruben was, meanwhile, he remembered that castaways often sink their rescuers, so he told Ruben that he would help him, but made Ruben promise that he would not grab him, because if so, they could sink together. Heroically, Miguel took Ruben to the strand where they met with their group. Once they were safe, Ruben requested Miguel not to tell what happened in the sea to the others, and Miguel accepted. In reciprocity, Ruben admitted to his friends that Miguel had won the race. Miguel said nothing, but he was totally glad and conscious that he had the way totally clear to his love, and also knew that the news of this legendary swimming competition would soon be known by Flora.

A teenage world

Even though the story is narrated from the perspective of a teenager, Vargas Llosa chose a third person omniscient narrator, who presents the events as they occur. Anyway, at the beginning of the story we find some analepsis (flashbacks) which allow the reader to know some events prior to the moment of the narration. The story begins to be narrated *in media res* (amidst), in the moment in which Miguel declares his love to Flora; from now on, we witness a story about learning, related to the meeting of the first love, which almost everyone finds in the youth years. This short story recreates the psychological environment in that time of life. It is a narration full of anguish, fear, drama, defiance, courage and love. As readers, at the beginning, we can feel Miguel's insecurity when he tries to declare his love, and then we feel his anguish when he receives Flora's answer. Later we witness the bar's atmosphere, when the young boys challenge each other and they finally have a showdown for the love of flora.

The characters are minimally described. Psychological aspect has a lot more of description than their looks, the only thing we know for sure is that Ruben is more stylized than Miguel, and we know nothing about the rest of the gang. Flora, the beautiful lady for which Miguel and Ruben have fell in love is, without intending it, the main motivation of the story, and is also almost a decorative character, because we do not know anything else about her after that brief dialogue with Miguel at the beginning of the story. The main characters of the story, Miguel and Ruben, suffer changes according to the situations. Once he has won the swimming race, according to *Melanes,* Miguel became a man, and the scared young boy with low self-esteem seems to have been left behind. On the other hand, we see that the change in Ruben is not that big, we always saw him as a very confident man, a total winner, but in the end, after his defeat, we see him more humble.

We can appreciate social relationships between young boys in depth. They have their own codes; their interactions, some of them surreptitious, are the ones which carry forward the action of the story. Let's remind, for example, Miguel knew that Ruben was going to declare his love to Flora, because the *Melanes* had told him. By the way, Miguel was being helped by Martha, his sister. Later on the story, in the bar, the group pressure leads to the realization of the beer drinking challenge, because at first, Ruben had thought about leaving the place. In the end, the friendship relations among the youth, sometimes authoritarian and even violent, trigger the outcome of the story, in which two young men defy each other to a swimming race, in winter, after having drunk a considerable amount of beer.

In addition to showing the teenager world in a masterful way, Vargas Llosa created a growing suspense in the story. The swimming race, considering the climatic conditions and the alcohol in the blood of the competitors, make the readers imagine the worst possible outcome. But in the last moment, the story gives a somehow unexpected turn, and it finishes with a sentence that unarguably shows a happy ending:

"There was a golden road in front of him".

AUGUSTO CÉSPEDES

The well

When the main objective is to quench thirst

Some pages taken from the Bolivian NCO Miguel Navajo's diary show the tragic reality of a group of Bolivian soldiers during the Chaco War. Reading these pages, we get to know the events that happen during the excavation of a dry well and the combat that takes place in order to claim it. After reading *The well*, we find that we have faced a masterpiece, which shows the most absurd side of a useless war.

By Fernando Chelle

About four months ago, I published a study on Augusto Roa Bastos' *The excavation,* included in the short story collection *Thunder among the leaves* (1953). In that short story, the Paraguayan Cervantes Prize winner tells the story of the prisoner Perucho Rodi, a Chaco War former fighter, whom is jailed in miserable conditions in Paraguay. Even though *The excavation* is about Rodi's struggle for freedom and the war is just a background, for it is only present in Rodi's hallucinations. Out there, in Gondra's front, he had excavated eighty meters from their trench to the back of the Bolivian rear, a successful strategy that took the Bolivians by surprise. But I will not analyze this short story again. My intention is just to use it as a reference because the story I will analyze has the same background, but it is approached from the Bolivian side.

The author I chose for this study is Augusto Céspedes (Cochabamba, Bolivia. February

6th, 1904 – La Paz, Bolivia. May 9th, 1997). I will analyze his short story *The well*, which belongs to his book *Sangre de mestizos*, published in Santiago de Chile in 1936 by Ediciones Ercilla. Both the book and the short story are considered "Ultimate jewels of the post war literature" by the aforementioned Augusto Roa Bastos.

Sangre de mestizos is Cespedes' first book. It was published immediately after the Chaco War was over. It is considered by most critics one of the best short story collections in Bolivian literature. We can say that Cespedes, who had an active role in that war -as a journalist for *El Universal* at first (1933-1944) and later as soldier (1934-1935)- wrote all of these stories during the war, from the rearguard or from the battlefront. It can be considered a cornerstone of the literature regarding to Chaco War, a recurrent topic among Bolivian and Paraguayan writers. The work consists of nine stories, in which a mestizo character always narrates in detail the reality of war. In these war-and-life stories, Cespedes shows the tragedies of war, the military tactics, and the weaknesses of the soldiers; he also makes social criticism and sometimes, even poetry.

Even though in the first lines of this article I referred to Roa Bastos' story in order to show the other side of the coin, in Cespedes' story the reader will find a deeper look into that absurd war between Paraguay and Bolivia. In the Bolivian's book, and in the particular short story, we meet an inhospitable land, with a warm and dry weather, deserted, covered exclusively by autochthonous trees, a place where there was no water and therefore the access to wells and lakes became an important part of the military strategy. The lack of a water source will be the backbone of the story that I will analyze, and it is mentioned by Eduardo Galeano in *Memoria del fuego (Memory of fire),* where he explains that the lack of water was precisely the soldier's cause of death.

Bolivia and Paraguay are at war. The poorest countries in South America, the ones that do not have access to the sea, those who have lost the most are killing each other for a piece of a map. Hidden beneath the creases of both flags, the Standard Oil Company and the Royal Dutch Shell are disputing over a probable oil of the Chaco. Stuck at war, both Bolivians and Paraguayans have the duty of hating each other in the name of a land that they do not love, that nobody loves; the Chaco is a gray desert, inhabited by spines and snakes, with no singing birds nor a single person's footprint. Everything is thirsty in this spooky land. The butterflies crowd in desperation around the few drops of water. Bolivians have come from a freezer to an oven: they have been taken from the Andean peaks and thrown to these burnt bushes. Here they are dying because of the bullets, but many more are dying of thirst. [5]

The well

Narrative structure

The text is divided in three parts, the second and the third part are led by a roman number, but the first part (I do not know why) is not, I do not know if it was Céspedes' decision not to number it, but the sure thing is it does not have a number. In its first part, Bolivian NCO Miguel Navajo is explaining his current situation and his decision of letting us know the story of a well, he chooses some excerpts of his personal diary that show the lives of some selfless zappers amidst an inhospitable waterless place, where they are threatened by the sun and dust. The first part of the story

---

[5] Eduardo Galeano, Memoria del Fuego, Montevideo, Del Chanchito, 1982

ends when they find a well, the main element of the second part. The second part of the story is the longest one, it starts on March 2nd. In this part we get to know about a group of Bolivian soldiers that have found a sterile well, from which they vainly try to drag some water, and we witness their hope and further misery. The third and last part of the story, which just quotes the date (December 7th), tells the bloody and unhappy ending of the defense of that well, useless like Chaco War itself.

Plot

The story reproduces some pages from Bolivian NCO Miguel Navajo's diary. In the beginning of the story, Navajo is the narrator of his current status: he says that he has been suffering of beriberi; he says he is a patient in the Tarairi Hospital, and he also informs that he was in the military campaign for two and a half years. He clarifies that, despite being sick and having been shot in his ribs last year, he is still captive and unable to go back to La

Paz. As he gets bored in the hospital, he reads his diary and decides to show us some of its excerpts. From now on, the style of the narration will change. In the second part, the narrator tells about the excavation of a well around 1933. The characters, including the narrator NCO, are part of the army's sapping line, which clear the roads for building bridges or digging ditches. So, the story does not make a clear reference to the enemy or the battles in this war, for thirst is the real enemy of these men. After receiving the order of digging a well from a man described as "blonde and short", the soldiers find an old and not deep hole, a hole that no one knows who dug and abandoned it. Then, the soldiers decided to keep digging that hole hoping to find some water, but the hole just keeps going deeper and deeper. For a moment, the soldiers feel hopeful because they found mud, but it happens to be just a layer of wet clay; as they go deeper, they only find dry soil. Twenty, thirty, and forty meters deep, they still cannot find the well, and the search for water becomes the real war, and it gets more real than the war being held on the surface. As they go deeper and deeper, the soldiers lose their notion of time; they just survive their thirst in perpetual darkness and begin to rave and faint because of the asphyxia. In a certain moment, the Paraguayans find out that the Bolivians have a well, but they are unaware it is a dry one. The Bolivian soldiers defend the well as if they were protecting something precious, as if it weren't a sterile well. The battle for the empty well lasts five hours and the death toll is thirteen soldiers, counting both sides. This useless battle for a useless well might work as a great metaphor for the absurdity of that war. The dry and sterile land ends up swallowing the soldiers' lives.

A brief final commentary

Undoubtedly, Cespedes' purpose in this story was to show how useless and pointless the Chaco Wars were. That dry well, which was only useful for burying both sides' soldiers, is a great symbol of that futility. The battle for that sterile well was not motivated for the will of getting some territory or the defense of an ideology; it was motivated by thirst, the survival instinct and also the stupidity of some and the ignorance of the others.

PABLO PALACIO

A man dead by kicks

When intolerance towards difference turns into violence

After reading a story in the Red Chronicle of the Diario de la Tarde (*Afternoon newspaper*), a citizen, who claims to be interested in justice, starts an investigation that leads him to some answers. From the first reading in the press, to the final reconstruction of the facts based on the speculations of the investigator, the story will show various topics, for example, media manipulation, desire, shame and the fears of an intolerant and violent society

By: Fernando Chelle

A man dead by kicks is a short story by Ecuadorian writer Pablo Palacio (Loja, Ecuador, February 25th 1906 – Guayaquil, Ecuador, January 7th 1947). This story is homonymous to the book published in 1927 by the Universidad Central's editorial in Quito. Besides being Palacio's most emblematic work, it is also one of the most representative stories of Ecuadorian literature.

A man dead by kicks (the book) is composed by nine stories, and most of them revolve around aspects related to the legal world. This was the first book by Pablo Palacio, who wrote it when he was just 20 years old after graduating as a lawyer; it is clearly visible that his academic studies where totally influential for him. Through a good use of narrative material, Palacio tries to provoke, sometimes with cynicism, sometimes with black humor, the local customs of the society of his time, exposing the privations of everyday life.

The story that I will analyze in depth revolves around aggression, violent behaviors and the social problems derived from the intolerance to different sexual options, in Quito by the times when Pablo Palacio lived. The story takes place in a historical era when homosexuality was qualified as a crime in Ecuador. From this starting point, there are some other secondary themes in the story, such as, for example, shame, concealment and tendentious media coverage.

In general lines the plot is: the character-narrator reads in the newspaper that a man was killed by kicks. Without giving details of the incident, the news say that the victim is "vicious." The narrator becomes obsessed in investigating the facts that led to the murder, but he only knows the fact that the man was "vicious"; besides that initial information, the investigator has two photographs that the Commissioner gave him. The investigation begins by establishing the vice that led

Octavio Ramírez (the man killed by kicking) to his tragic end. In the end, the narrator-character speculates (and is carried away by his imagination), concluding that Octavio Ramírez was homosexual and that the father of the young boy had killed him because Ramírez had harassed his 14-year-old son.

We can divide the internal structure of the story in eight small moments, and each one of them has a specific point of interest.

1) The information of the Red Chronicle shown in the newspaper. 2) Narrator's decision to investigate 3) Narrator chooses his investigation methodology. 4) The vice. 5) Photos. 6) The investigative study. 7) The conclusion of the investigator – narrator. 8) Reconstruction of the facts.

The story begins with the reproduction of a news story. The narrator-character shows the readers the news as he read it in the red chronicle of the Diario de la Tarde, so we become witnesses of the material on which he will investigate later in the story. This is the first moment of the story's internal structure; it is the only one that is narrated in third person, because the voice is the reproduction of the newspaper. Take for example: *"We will try to keep our readers up to date on what is known about this mysterious death"*.

The facts in the news are told prior to the development of the action of the story; the narrator-character reads the news the day after the death happened. The red chronicle begins with the words "last night" and in the second paragraph, it says "this morning". The report in particular refers to the words of Ramírez, who claimed to have been the victim of a beating by some people after having asked for a cigarette. The incident took place between the streets Escobedo and García, and then the injured was taken to the police. In the second paragraph of this first segment, where Ramírez is already mentioned deceased, we can find the most important statement of the story, since the narrator begins the investigation from it: *"The only thing that could be known, by an accidental fact, is that the deceased was vicious "*.

The interest of the narrator-character in clarifying the facts is seen in the tracking he does to the case in search of information in the news. But he does not decide to start the investigation immediately; he decides to start it after ten days have passed. From this moment, the time of the action story coincides with the time of the narration. The first singular person is used from that moment until the end, the narrative voice is taken by the character-narrator, a homodiegetic narrator (the narrator tells the story from the inside), and also autodiegetic (the narrator is a character). The narrator is determined to find out, without leaving his home, the reasons that moved some guys to attack another person by kicking. The fact that the narrator laughs to satisfaction and that the death of a person in that circumstance seems funny to him is a signal that this character-narrator has a quite particular psychological complexity. He says he wanted to carry out an experimental study of the event and then discarded that possibility, because it seems more interesting to him to study the reasons that led those individuals to act in the way they did. Once that point is solved, he will light his pipe (in an Arthur Conan Doyle style), which will become a leitmotif in the story, and then he begins to investigate. So we move to the third moment of the internal structure of the story, which focuses on the methodology that will be used in the investigation. The character-narrator is partial to the inductive method, which starts from the least known to the best known information, because in reality he knows little of the fact he wants to investigate, a very good reason to not try to deduce.

The character-narrator is determined to investigate, but even after having chosen the methodology, remains paralyzed for a moment without knowing what to do. After reading again the Diario de la Tarde, on January 13th, he notices the fundamental fact: "*The only thing that could be known, by an accidental fact, is that the deceased was vicious.*" The interpretation of this data (which the investigator seems to have resolved intuitively at the end of this fourth moment) will unleash the following events of the story.

The fifth moment of the story focuses on the search for the truth, and the two photographs are important here because those pictures, and the fact that Ramírez was vicious, are the only elements that the character-narrator has, to carry out the investigation. The scenery changes, the action takes place in the 6th Police Station, but the commissioner, apart from providing the photos, does not help with the investigation because it does not give concrete answers about the characteristics of the deceased.

In the sixth moment we witness a new change of scenery, the action returns to the house of the character-narrator. There, he locks himself in the studio, lights his pipe back on and focuses on the analysis of the photographs. After reviewing repeatedly both pictures, he makes a drawing of the deceased that has feminine characteristics, and that is the moment when he confirms which was his vice. This leads him to insist that Ramírez was in fact a bad person, showing again the psychological complexity of this character. This moment ends with the words of the protagonist, repeating the central question of his investigation: "*I tried ... I was trying to know why he was killed; Yes, why they killed him ...*"

Immediately after the character-narrator repeats this question, the story takes a somewhat radical turn and we witness the investigator's conclusions, which will be the center of interest of the seventh segment. He is convinced that Ramírez lied, because it is illogical that someone is attacked this way just for asking for a cigarette. Ramírez surely had lied because he could not tell the truth and this was surely related to his vice. From that certainty, the character-narrator raises and discards different assumptions. Then, from some real and other just possible elements, reconstructs the personality of Ramírez.

In the eighth and last segment of the story, which focuses on the reconstruction of the events that have taken place, the writer retakes the journalistic tone of the beginning of the story; the difference is that the information handled in this moment is a total assumption. The character-narrator makes a reference to the place where Ramírez lived, then pictures him lustful, full of desire, altered by his passions, until he reaches the place where the attack takes place. Ramírez, victim of his needs, after flirting with some men with whom he meets fortuitously, seeks to satisfy his desires with a 14-years-old boy. The young man, after being grabbed by Ramírez, screams for the help of his father, a large worker who comes back after hearing his son screaming; the narrator-character had previously described the worker, noting the wide heels of his shoes. After questioning and insulting Ramírez, the worker kicks him three fatal times. In this last segment, the complex psychology of the character-narrator (who found the story funny the first time he read it and got angry with Ramirez when discovered what his vice was) gets on the side of the aggressor and enjoys the cruel attack, which ultimately leads to the death of Octavio Ramírez.

As a conclusion

In successive passages of this analysis I referred to the psychological complexity of the character-narrator, a complexity that we could link to an unhealthy personality. The conclusion this character (who claims to be interested in justice) makes, is one of many possible, since his research was based primarily on conjectures, speculations and assumptions. The story reproduced in the first moment of the story is not clear, allows speculation, and that is what the character-narrator used, stating the "vice" of Ramírez as the driving force of his investigation.

The brilliance of Pablo Palacio in this story, besides the creation of that complex and particular character-narrator, can be seen in the way he transmitted the desires, passions and torments of Ramirez, the fear of the 14-years-old boy and the anger of his father, the worker from Quito.

¿Has mankind advanced in the social integration of people with different sexual preferences?

Obviously, since the date of its publication to date, society has made much progress, but there is still much to do, so people like Ramirez do not live the tragedy of being condemned by those who fear, marginalize or reject everything which is different from what is socially accepted as valid due to prejudices.

FRANCISCO MASSIANI

A gift for Julia

When insecurity and fear prevail, the end is always sad

A boy in love must choose a very special gift for his dream girl. With just a few bucks, he must surprise her, seduce her, and make her fall in love. After studying different options, he decides to gift the girl a chicken, but in the end, fear plays a trick on him.

By: Fernando Chelle

A gift for Julia is a short story by Venezuelan writer Francisco Massiani (Caracas, Venezuela, 1944), born François Massiani Antonietti and popularly known as Pancho Massiani. The story is part of the book *Las primeras hojas de la noche (1970)* published in Caracas by Monte Ávila Editores. This book, as well as his short story collection *El llanero solitario tiene la cabeza pelada como un cepillo de dientes* (1975) has been very popular in his country since its publication. The reason for its popularity may be that it can reach a wide range of readers. Most of the protagonists in these stories are teenagers facing the problems of life for the first time. Generally, Massiani's short stories have a first person narrator (as in the analyzed text) that shows us a colloquial, emotive and sometimes humoristic language, typical of the teenage years. And the teenage world is precisely the prime matter in Massiani's stories: their first moments of happiness and sadness of the daily life.

The main topic of the story is insecurity, embodied in the actions carried out by the main character. In short, the argument can be resumed like this: Juan, a hesitant young man, faces the difficulty of choosing a birthday gift for his friend Julia, of whom he is in love (although he does not express it explicitly). His inexperience and improvisation lead him to gift her with a chicken, a gift that he does not dare to give her in the end. Juan, who is both the protagonist and the narrator of the story, refers some past events to the readers.

The story begins with a brief meditation about the reason that triggers the action: the choice of the gift for Julia. Then, in what we can state as a second moment of an internal structure of the story, he refers to the visit he paid to the girl's house, a visit prior to her birthday, which will make the readers know the characteristics of the two main characters, and also the characteristics of Carlos, a character that is mentioned in the narrative. This moment ends when Julia and the protagonist come to an agreement of meeting the next day at three thirty in the cafeteria. The third moment of the internal structure takes place the day after the visit, that is, on the day of the meeting. This segment tells Jorge's journey through different places and also his meditation, in the search of the right gift. It is here when he sees a rabbit and thinks that the ideal gift for Julia would be a chicken. Once Juan has the right gift in his hands, we move on to the fourth and last moment of the narrative, the longest and most tense part of the story: the moment of the date in the cafeteria

The object that will trigger the action of the story and that occupies the meditations of the protagonist in the first two paragraphs of the text, is already present in the title of the work. "A gift for Julia", is an emblematic title, which advances in the main topic of the story and shows what the role of the protagonist will be, because although the name of the girl appears in the title, the story is actually about the psychological processes and the personal universe of the young protagonist, aspects that will be known in depth. It is not even necessary that we finish the first paragraph of the story to realize that it is narrated in a very natural way. The narrative voice, in first person, is the voice of the teenager who, far from any aestheticism, chooses to express himself in the colloquial and daily language of young Venezuelans. After making a brief meditation about what would be a good gift for Julia, Juan makes a reference to Carlos, a young man who will be an antagonist in the story, but who will only appear referred, and never takes part in the actions of the story. In any case, Carlos is described, as a rude young man, somewhat more experienced than Juan; but perhaps the fundamental trait of the character, what characterizes him most, is that he also aspires to be Julia's boyfriend. There is no physical description of this absent character, but neither is there any of Juan or

Julia, this is a story where there is a prevalence of the psychological traits of the characters over their physical traits.

While choosing the elements that he will tell the readers, Juan decides to tell about the visit he paid to Julia. There, the readers will get to know the personality, of both Juan and Julia. Juan's personality will be more deeply known because, as a narrator, he will be responsible for showing us how his thinking develops as the events happen. He is a very direct narrator, he permanently has his readers in mind and there are moments when he even explains why he chooses to refer to a certain fact. For example, when he says "*And I was still playing the drum. That's what I tell you so you can see.* ". Julia is shown as a distracted girl, but not at all naive, she likes to show off, making previously rehearsed seductive poses. Carlos, the antagonist boy, who also aspires to Julia's love, is a great shadow in Juan's thoughts and also works as a great projected shadow in the story, since he will never be present in the action, he only appears when he is referenced. Although Juan never expresses explicitly being in love with Julia throughout the story, there are moments in the narration that evidence it, for example, this:

"When that happens, when she smiles to me, then I take my chance to watch her little mouth, those two little orange pieces, because that's the way it is: she has two little orange pieces, and I know for example that her upper lip, when separated from the lower one, it seems that it was afraid to leave the other one alone, and then it trembles a little bit, not a lot, just a little, and then it approaches the other and accompanies it a little and then, from between the two little orange pieces, comes out something like a little drop juice that stains a little the wrinkles of her lips and then I feel dizzy, and I feel a sensation of having something like chewing

*gum between my molars and she looks at me
and says:*

-What's wrong?

*And I wake up. I know I would never be able
to hold her hand, ever. "*

This passage, besides adding lyricism to the
story, shows the main characteristics of Juan,
his fear, his lack of audacity to face the
situations and carry out his desires.

Like most young people, Juan just has the
money his mother gives him to satisfy his
needs. With that few money, he leaves his
house and tries to find the gift for the girl and
ends up buying a chicken, as mentioned
before, something very unusual. Perhaps his
choice has something to with the fact that,
since Julia belongs to a family with a good
economic position (something we know from
the amount of service personnel she has in
her house), Juan wants to seduce her with a

gift that is not important for its material value, but for its sentimental value. In short, perhaps that, his inexperience, or an impulse, made him think that a chicken would be a great idea for a unique and special gift-

After having the wanted gift in his hands, he goes to the place where he was scheduled to meet Julia at three thirty in the afternoon, at the cafeteria. There he asks for a chocolate milkshake and feels annoyed by the place's waiter, who does not stop watching the box moving because of the chicken inside. As it was almost four o'clock and the girl was not showing up, he decides to call her home, but she is not there; the girl's mother, with whom he has a brief conversation, tells him that she had left. After Juan is annoyed again by the waiter, who just asked him directly about the receiver of the gift, that is, who was supposed to get the chicken, Julia arrives. The arrival of the girl is almost cinematographic: she gets down of an impressive black Buick with a spotted dress and gets all the looks of the men who were in the cafeteria. The impact of her arrival, the jealousy he feels because of the looks on Julia and the nerves of the moment make Juan "feel uncomfortable", Juan takes the chicken out of the box and hides it in the pocket of his jacket. The first thing Julia asks is if he has been there for a long time, but Juan, full of fear, feels intimidated and lies saying that he had just arrived. From now on, we witness the psychological and physical struggle of the protagonist, as he is forced to face the situation with the chicken in his pocket. His nerves, being forced to keep the arm in the same position so that the chicken would not scream, and having to answer Julia's questioning about the empty box, were factors that combined caused Juan to end up decompensating. Anyway, also at this moment of the story, Massiani manages to introduce one of those almost lyrical passages with which he manages to show the boy's infatuation:

"Then she ran her tongue through her mouth, wiped the stain of Coke on her lips, and stared at me, smiling. Immediately I began to feel lost. As if I was being lifted from the ground. Far and at the same time very close, so much, that I could count the moles on her nose, those little brown or sometimes pink points that she has in her nose, and the more I looked at her, the more she smiled and I flew further away from her, with her smile, without it, with the smile alone, floating in the air, with her smile of red foam, and after that she had flown with her smile, her smile was returning to her face, covered her entire face and I realized that I was there, in front of her, and I felt a sweet little fear in my belly. It was a little fear like when we go in a car and suddenly the car reaches a rise, and falls, and you feel something, something opens up in your belly, and your belly fills up with that sweet fear that you feel afterwards it escapes from you and leaves you empty, as with a strange hunger. "

Then, when Julia insistently asks Juan what is happening to him, because she notices his physical decompensation, he becomes annoyed and changes his emotions in a radical way. From that moment, he will no longer defend the helpless Julia from Carlos "the bigmouth", but quite the opposite. Juan, feeling that his dreams are gone, thinks about serving the girl to her antagonist so that he can do with her even worse things than the ones he had thought about before.

Julia's departure from the cafeteria is very similar to her entrance; she is getting all the looks with her provocative moves, she gets on the black Buick and gets away. Juan did not even have time to meditate on why these things happened, because the waiter came to his table again to ask if he had been afraid to give the girl the chicken. He did not know what to do; he only managed to put his head in his arms. The waiter went away and, along with a fat person who was in the place, began to mock Juan, which leads to the protagonist's cry, because he felt that everything was lost already and nothing mattered. The story ends when the boy takes the chicken out of his pocket and, after some confusing first impressions, finds out, terrified, that the animal has died.

An anecdote by Massiani himself, which I think is relevant

Some time ago, watching some videos of and about Francisco Massiani on Youtube, I found a testimony by the author himself, a very interesting one by the way. The video, uploaded by Juan Carlos Carrano Henríquez titled "*El día que no conocí a Cortázar (The day I did not meet Cortazar)*", is a recording made to the Venezuelan author at his home in La Florida (Caracas), where he tells about the day he went to meet Cortázar. In the video, Massiani says that in the month of March of 1969, when he was living in Paris, at the Hotel Wepper, he received a phone call from photographer Antonio Gálvez who told him that Julio Cortázar wanted to meet him because he had read an article wrote by Massiani and published in *Imagen Magazine*, entitled "After Gálvez ", an article Cortazar had loved.

The meeting was supposed to take place on Friday at four in the afternoon at the apartment of Antonio Gálvez. Massiani went there, but, similar to what happened to the character in his fiction, he did not make the final move, he did not knock on the door and ended up going back to his hotel, therefore the meeting with Cortázar never happened. I find this anecdote very significant because it is an almost contemporary event to the fiction of "*A gift for Julia*", published just one year after that event. The fear that seized Juan in the fiction is the same that seized his creator in real life.

Index

Made in the USA
Middletown, DE
15 December 2022

18694235R00136